European Classics
for Men

First published in 1994 by Absolute Classics, an imprint of Absolute Press, 14 Widcombe Crescent, Bath, England.

Cover and text design: Ian Middleton

Computer output and copy editing: Andrew McLeish

Printed by The Longdunn Press Ltd, Bristol

Absolute
Monologues

European Classics
for Men

ABSOLUTE CLASSICS

Contents

Preface

I

In only five years, the independent Absolute Classics has published over seventy plays from the European classic repertoire. Most of these plays – in translation – have received important productions on the modern stage. Seen in the playhouses of the Royal Shakespeare Company and the Royal National Theatre, throughout the world with Cheek by Jowl and other touring companies, in the intimacy of that room above a London pub – the Gate Theatre, Notting Hill – the plays have attracted widespread critical acclaim and popularity amongst theatre-goers. They are all translated and adapted by Britain's leading dramatists, giving a dynamic contemporary voice to classic theatre.

Absolute Classics pioneer the rediscovered, the British première; thus the plays hold an extra fascination. A collection of monologues is a treasure-trove of the European repertoire: from the Greeks to the 20th Century. Monologues are touchstones. They inspire you to explore the complete play from where each character comes.

The monologues selected here are presented in a rough historical order, period by period, playwright to playwright, play to play. They contain a diverse range of moods, atmospheres, histrionics, wit and comedy. For quick reference, the act, scene and page numbers from the Absolute Classics edition are noted; and they are loosely labelled: comedy, dark comedy, light serious and serious, as a guide-at-a-glance. The monologues actually mix the introspective, the extrovert, the self-consciously theatrical, the soliloquy, the descriptive, the compelling, the orated. A monologue is both dependent on its context and yet independent of it. They can be self-contained units, existing in their own right. Above all a monologue is to be enjoyed for the immediacy of its language, its situation, its character − its performance. A great monologue captures the essence of character in the moment.

At first sight, some monologues seem more immediate than others. A knowingly ironic speech from a comic servant is clearly appealing. However, a complex tragic soliloquy will be just as rewarding.

We have abridged as little as possible, but you might choose to cut and mould a piece to your own individual taste. If you're using a monologue for an audition, then it's worth bearing in mind the adage that less is more.

Ultimately, a monologue will speak for itself.

II

When Bath's best publisher, Jon Croft, invited us to create the series Absolute Monologues we were, of course, flattered. As dramaturg and actress we were given *carte blanche* to cut swathes through the great dramatic voices of Western theatre. It was an exciting project; but it was also pretty daunting.

Yet having been involved in the commissioning of some of these translations as Literary Manager of the Gate Theatre, and having played in some of them, such as Rosaura in Calderón's *Life's a Dream* (La Vida es Sueño), we appreciated their blend of classic text with (often cheeky) contemporary voice. And as theatre-goers, we have all seen the majority of these plays on stage in the past ten years. They are a familiar part of our generation's repertoire, a generation at ease with its hybrid sense of nationhood and conscious of its pan-European heritage.

It's this broader perspective which partly gives writers the confidence to work with material from countries in whose language they may not be fluent. Though most of the dramatists represented here *do* translate from the original, a few offer versions of a play. Nick Dear, for instance, freely admits he knew no more Russian than 'vodka' when he wrote his version of Ostrovsky's *A Family Affair* (Svoi Lyudi – Sochtsemsya!) for Cheek by Jowl. It's a joyously theatrical version, probably more true to the scurrilous spirit of Ostrovsky than any painstaking 'literal' might be. After all, it's for the theatre that these plays are produced, not for the library.

Neil Bartlett is a performer, director, novelist and translator who speaks fluent French. Translating Racine and Molière he says: 'My work has always been concerned with reinventing the past as a way of articulating the present'. And with characteristic theatricality he proclaims: 'Let us be grand' – 'If translations are to be faithful, they cannot be literal. My translations are very faithful'. The Spanish translator and adaptor David Johnston coined a phrase for this: 'faithful infidelity'. Translations are as much about the modern interpreter's distinctive voice as they are about the original writer's. Ranjit Bolt's Corneille couplets ping out at you; Noel Clark's draw you in.

While we must thank all the writers – both living and dead – whose work is represented here, we must also acknowledge all responsibility for any misrepresentation. As far as possible, Jon Croft has helped us avoid any howlers: he's been an encouraging and good-natured guide throughout our journey. Helpful hints also came from Graham Anderson, Laurence Boswell, Kenneth McLeish, Timothy Walker, Clive Brill, Oscar Ceballos and Toby Jones.

The *frisson* between original writer and his modern interpreter is knowingly summed up in the opening banter between a Duke and his two comic side-kicks in Lope de Vega's *Lost in a Mirror* (El Castigo sin Venganza), adapted by Adrian Mitchell:

Duke: Enough nonsense, you fool.

Febo: Sir, he'll feel better for
          Having a metaphor,
          He's of the fashionable school.

Ricardo: You don't like modern poetry?
          Please accept my apology
          Lock me up in an anthology –
          Throw away the key.

Duke: I don't like verse based on pretence.
          I want reality and playfulness,
          A good story and seriousness –
          But you're all simile and no sense.

In one sense, theatre is only a simile for reality. Yet we can only know what reality is *like* by articulating it through our imaginations. And the the most exciting creative arena for that is theatre.

Simon Reade & Alison Reid
London, 1994

Greek Drama: Euripides

The three Greek tragedians of the 5th Century BC –
Aeschylus, Sophocles and the wilder Euripides – use the
mythological past as a perspective on their own historical
present. The stories and plots upon which their tragedies are
based were well-known to contemporary audiences. The
religious and cultural heritage was laid down in Homeric times
(10th Century BC). What was new was the way the stories
were told and the attitude taken by the playwrights.

Euripides is far more sardonic than his predecessors. His
obsession with the Trojan War in particular shows him using
the desolation of its aftermath as a no-man's-land of human
frailty. Fractured morals and shattered ethics – the human
consequences of war – are laid bare in the ruins of Troy.

Euripides' writing reflects the concerns of his subjects, using
single words to express a range of feeling. The translator
Kenneth McLeish identifies Euripides' style as allowing the
actor 'a great deal of creative space'. McLeish also retains some
of the original exclamations, such as 'Fe-oo' (often translated
melodramatically in the past as 'Alas!' or 'Alack!

McLeish's pared down translations have been partly responsible
for revitalising Greek tragedy for a new generation: Cheek by
Jowl's *Philoctetes*; the Manchester Royal Exchange's *Medea*; the
Deborah Warner/Fiona Shaw RSC production of *Electra*; the
Gate Theatre's Trojan plays directed by Katie Mitchell and
Laurence Boswell.

While these are some of the greatest classical roles of Greek
antiquity, they are living characters, immediate, who touch the
raw nerves of hope and despair.

Women of Troy
(TROADES)

EURIPIDES 414 BC
translated by Kenneth McLeish 1991

Menelaus and the Greeks have destroyed Troy. It was Melenaus'
wife, Helen, who was stolen by Paris (son of Queen Hecuba and
King Priam of Troy) and thus cursed by both sides as the cause of the
Trojan War. Menelaus is now preparing to confront her.

MENELAUS
  Bright sunshine! Happy day,
  When Menelaus lays hands on ... *her* again.
  To suffer so, for such a wife!
  They think I came to Troy for her.
  Not so. I came for him, that guest no-guest
  Who lodged in my palace and stole my wife.
  The price is paid, God saw to that:
  That man and his country, by Greek spears dead.
  Now I come for her, the Spartan –
  I still can't speak her name and smile.
  She's mine, tagged here with all the other spoil.
  The men who risked their lives for her
  Have handed her to me.
  I can kill her here or ship her home.
  Helen! Hell to her native land!
  I'll cargo her home
  To death, to pay the price
  For so many friends, so many loved ones, lost.
  Bring her out here. Drag her:
  That hair, scabbed with dead men's blood.
  As soon as the winds blow fair, we'll take her home.

Hecuba
(EKABE)

EURIPIDES 424 BC
translated by Kenneth McLeish 1992

Hecuba's son, **Polydorus**, was sent to Thrace by his father, Priam,
when the Greeks threatened Troy. He was sheltered by Priam's ally
Polymestor. Now Troy is destroyed and Priam is dead, Polymestor
kills Polydorus for the gold his father sent with him as security.

   The Ghost of Polydorus has begged the gods of the underworld to
remain in limbo for Hecuba to discover his body and give him a
proper burial.

No-man's-land, before the ruins of Troy.

POLYDORUS' GHOST
   You see Polydorus, son of Queen Hecuba,
   Son of Priam. From folds of the Underworld
   I come, from gates of Night,
   Where Hades rules, in exile from the gods.
   I was a child, too young to shoulder arms
   Or wear a sword. My father's city, Troy,
   Was threatened by Greek might. He sent me,
   In secret, here to Thrace, to an old ally,
   Polymestor, who rules these farms, these fields.
   The people breed horses. Polymestor rules,
   Their spear-lord. So here I came,
   And with me my father smuggled gold:
   If Troy fell, his sons would still not starve.
   So far, so good. Troy's towers survived.
   My brother, Hector, kept his city safe.
   I grew up here in Thrace, at Polymestor's court,
   Grew like a sapling – doomed.
   Greeks snatch the life of Troy, snatch Hector's life,
   Storm the palace, slaughter Priam my father

At his own altar. Blood; butchery; Achilles' son.
News reaches Thrace. My father's good old friend
Kills me for the gold, to keep the gold,
And dumps my carcass. There on the shore I roll,
Roll on the tide-line, unwept, unburied.
Three days now. My flesh an empty shell.
My spirit here, hovering. My mother's here,
Unhappy Hecuba. A prisoner-of-war in Thrace.
The whole Greek fleet sits here, waiting,
Here on these beaches. They were dipping oars,
Stirring the sea for home, when Achilles' ghost appeared,
There on his grave-mound, demanding, demanding
His share of honour, blood-sacrifice.
He demands Polyxena my sister, her life-blood.
He'll get it. They're his friends, they'll honour him.
My sister dies, today; it's fate. And Hecuba?
Two bodies, two children dead, she'll see,
My unhappy mother: Polyxena's first, then mine.
They'll find me. A slave-woman will find me,
Flotsam, sea-sodden; they'll bury me.
I begged this favour from the powers below:
A grave, my own mother's hands to bury me.
It's granted, all I asked for, granted.

She's coming. There, from Agamemnon's tent.
Old, afraid. I appeared to her, she's terrified.
Fe-oo.
Hecuba, how are you fallen! Royal palace then,
The dust of slavery now. Some god looked down on you,
Saw how high your pride, and gave you this.

Hecuba
(EKABE)

EURIPIDES 424 BC
translated by Kenneth McLeish 1992

Talthybius is the messenger of the Greek army. He has witnessed
the grief endured by the women of Troy during the wars. Queen
Hecuba has lost her husband and children, one by one. Lastly, her
youngest child Polyxena is sacrificed to Achilles. Talthybius has the
painful task of reporting a daughter's death to the mother.

TALTHYBIUS

Lady, I wept before, when I watched her die.
Now you ask me to tell it, I'll weep again.

There, gathered at the graveside,
The whole Greek army, to watch the sacrifice.
I was close by.
Achilles' son took Polyxena's hand,
Led her on to the mound, left her.
A detachment of men, hand-picked,
In case the victim struggled. Achilles' son
Took a golden cup, lifted it,
Poured an offering to his father. Signed to me
To call for silence. Up I stepped.
'Greeks! Be quiet! Be calm! Be still!'
No sound. The whole crowd – still.
He said, 'Achilles, father, accept this offering,
Come up from the Underworld. Dark blood,
Virgin blood, drink it, it's yours,
Our gift to you, from me, from every Greek.
Smile on us. Watch us, and smile on us,
As we hoist our anchors and sail for home.
Grant us safe journey. Home!' He finished.
The army echoed his prayer. He drew

His sword, the gold inlay. He signed
To the execution party: hold her.
She saw what they intended. 'Greeks' she said,
'You sacked my city. I die of my own free will.
Don't touch me. I won't flinch, won't struggle.
Let me die freely, go free to the Underworld.
A princess – don't make me a slave among the dead.
Don't shame me.' The soldiers heard and cheered.
Lord Agamemnon told them to let her go.
Then, then, she took her dress, ripped it
From neck to navel. She showed her breasts,
Her midriff, beautiful as a statue.
She slipped to her knees. Achilles' son.
She spoke her bravest, saddest words of all.
'Choose, prince. Here, if you will – my heart –
Or here – my throat. I'm ready. Stab.'
He pitied her. He was reluctant, eager, all at once.
He cut her windpipe. Fountain of blood.
She was dying. And still she took good care
To fall modestly, to hide what no man should see.
Her soul left her body. At once, bustle.
The whole army, busy. Some gather leaves
To strew the body. Some fetch logs, to make a pyre.
Those who stood with empty hands were jeered.
'For shame! Bring gifts. Clothes, ornaments.
She was noble, brave, a princess, unmatched.'

That's how she died, lady. No mother on Earth
Could boast a better child, or harsher fate.

Hecuba
(EKABE)

EURIPIDES 424 BC
translated by Kenneth McLeish 1992

Polymestor was given charge of Hecuba and Priam's son,
Polydorus, when Greece first threatened Troy. Now that Troy has
been destroyed, Priam murdered, and Hecuba taken captive,
Polymestor has killed Polydorus for his gold. One by one, Hecuba's
children have been taken from her, or murdered. When she finds
that her former ally, Polymestor, has killed her last remaining son,
she lures him to her tent – where the women of Troy attack him,
blind him, and murder his own sons. Hearing his 'howling; yelling',
Agamemnon, the Greek leader, runs to discover what has happened:
'Control yourself. You're like a wild animal.
Speak sensibly, calmly. I'll hear you'.

POLYMESTOR

Listen. There was a child: Polydorus,
Their youngest son, hers and Priam's.
Priam sent him from Troy to me,
Suspected that Troy would fall, sent him to me
For safety. I killed him. I'll tell you why –
Good reasons, common sense. If he lived,
Your enemy, if he survived, he'd gather Troy,
Rebuild it; you Greeks would hear
That one of Priam's sons still lived; you'd make
Another expedition, land here in Thrace,
Plunder. Disaster for Troy's neighbours.
We had it before. Agamemnon...?

She heard he was dead. She sent for me. Some tale
Of gold, Priam's gold, a hoard of it in Troy.
No one else was to know. She took me in there. My sons.
I sat on a couch. Lay back. The women beside me.

This side, that side. Conversation, politeness.
'Such wonderful weave, your cloak. May we see it
Against the light? And these are Thracian spears?'
So they stripped me of both. Unarmed.
Others picked up my sons, dandled them,
Passed them to one another – away from their father.
Then, suddenly, politeness ends. Daggers –
Where from? Their clothes? They stab the boys.
I'm held. Arms, legs. They grip like an octopus.
I try to get up, to help the children. They grab my hair.
My arms, gripped to my sides. Outnumbered.
Then – horrible, horrible – they take pins,
Brooches, stab my eyes, blood, pulp.
They hide. They run away. I'm a wild beast, springing,
Scrabbling after them, wild dogs, a hunter,
Battering, smashing.

That's what they did. I helped you, Agamemnon,
I killed your enemy – and that's what they did to me.
I've one more thing to say. Whatever names men find
For women, now, in the past, in future time,
Come down to this: they're monsters, unheard of,
Unique on land, on sea. Who sees them, knows it.

Orestes

EURIPIDES 408 BC
translated by Kenneth McLeish 1993

Orestes and his sister Electra have murdered their mother,
Clytemnestra, because not only did she take a lover while their father
Agamemnon was in Troy winning the war for the Greeks, but she
then murdered Agamemnon on his return. They await trial for
vengeful matricide. Hardened by the terror of what they have
endured and what they have done, they exude an amoral arrogance.
Here Orestes puts his case to Tyndareus, his grandfather,
Clytemenstra's father, who says:
> *'How dare you? Bluster. Insolence.*
> *Smart answers to make me smart'.*

ORESTES

My lord ... grandfather ... I'm embarassed.
You'll be furious, hurt, whatever I say.
Respect for you, respect for one's elders...
I must put it aside. I have to speak.

To kill your own mother, and break the law;
To avenge your own father, and keep the law –
What sort of choice is that? My father sowed the seed,
Your daughter accepted it, carried it, ripened it.
I thought, without a father there can be no child;
I took his side, my creator, not hers, my nurse.
In any case, your daughter – I won't call her my mother –
Made ... private bed-arrangements ... with another man.
I blush to mention it – her shame is mine – but still –≠
She had a private bedmate, here in the house, Aegisthus.
I killed him first, then her. Was I breaking the law, or
   keeping it?

You want me stoned for what I did. I say it helped all
  Greece.
What if all mothers took to murdering their husbands,
Baring their breasts to their children, begging for mercy –
And getting away with it? They'd kill their men for fun.
You call me an animal, but I put a stop to that.
I despised her, I killed her, and I was right –
A woman who kissed her man goodbye to the Trojan War
And ran straight to a lover's bed; knew what it meant,
Didn't blush, didn't kill herself when she was caught
But waited till he came home, my father, killed him instead.

Ye gods – excuse me for bringing gods into this –
What else was I supposed to do? Keep quiet?
What would he have done, the victim? He'd have cursed
  me,
He'd be capering, here, now, with his Furies, his witches.
Or does only she have Furies? Are there none for him,
Her victim? It's your fault, grandfather. You destroyed me.
You fathered her. She was yours, that foulness
Who stole my father and made me murder her.
You've heard of Odysseus' wife, Penelope?
Her son doesn't murder her, and why? Because
She sleeps alone, no lovers stain her bed.
You've heard of Apollo? At the navel of the Earth
He gives clear prophecies, not to be denied.
His orders. He told me, 'Kill'; I killed –
So exile him, kill him, his blame not mine.
What else was I to do? He ordered it; I did it;
If I can't trust him now, where else can I turn?

What was done was well done. It turned out well –
Except for me who did it. How happy they are
Whose marriages are happy. How cursed they are,
What laughing-stocks they are, whose wives are whores.

Orestes

EURIPIDES 408 BC
translated by Kenneth McLeish 1993

Orestes and Electra have killed their mother, Clytemnestra, because she took a lover while her husband Agamamnon was winning the Trojan War for the Greeks and *then* killed Agamemnon on his return. Orestes, who was instructed by the god Apollo to seek vengeance, goes on trial before the people and war heroes of Argos. Here the **Old Man** recounts the proceedings to Electra.

OLD MAN
As it happened, I'd just come into town.
I'm a countryman, work in the fields.
I wanted to know how things were with you
And Orestes. (I worked for your father once,
In the old days, your family looked after me,
Old loyalty.) There was a crowd, climbing the hill
Where Danaus and Aegyptus, years ago,
Called the people to settle that argument.
I asked someone, 'What is it? What's going on?
Some enemy approaching?' *He* said, 'Look:
Orestes. Over there. Can't you see? His trial's today.'
He was right. I never expected to see such a sight,
Such a pitiful sight: Orestes, Pylades,
Your brother tottering with sickness,
Pylades supporting him, helping him along
As if *he* was his brother, or his nurse.

The rest of the people gathered. Silence.
'In the case of Orestes the matricide,
Who wants to speak?' Talthybius stood up –
He was with your father at the sack of Troy.
Sucking up to those in power, as usual.
Praised your father, didn't praise your brother,

Cat's cradle of arguments, 'dangerous precedent' –
All the time fawning on Aegisthus' men.
Typical functionary. No views of your own,
Choose the people in power and lick their boots.

Diomedes was next. Prince Diomedes.
He wasn't for killing you, either of you;
Banishment, he said – far more appropriate.
Well, some of them cheered, and others booed.
Up jumps another one, a mouth on legs,
You know the type, loud, crude, 'a simple citizen' –
'Stone 'em,' he said, 'Nothing to it. Stone 'em.'
Your grandad Tyndareus put him up to that.
Someone else stood up, said exactly the opposite.
No conman this time, an honest face,
Not the kind who hangs around street corners,
A working man, a farmer, salt of the earth,
Decent, clean-living, listens to all the arguments
And then makes up his own mind. *He* said
Orestes, lord Agamemnon's son, deserved
A medal for what he'd done, avenging his father,
Killing that bitch, hated by the gods, who'd tried
To steal all we had. Who'd go to war, he said,
Who'd ever leave home to fight,
If *that's* what happened to their wives?
A patter of applause: the family men.

No one else comes forward. Your brother's turn.
'People of Argos,' he says, 'It was for all your sakes,
Not just for my father's, that I killed my mother.
If we say it's legal for wives to kill their husbands,
Which man of us is safe? We'd be in their hands.
Don't do it. She betrayed my father, and died for it.
If you kill me now, the law stands on its head,
They'll do as they like, you're all as good as dead.'

Fine words, but they weren't about to listen.
The loudmouth was shouting, 'Death!' A show of hands.

He won. Orestes – what could he do? – persuaded them
To put down their stones. 'By my own hand I'll die,'
He said. 'Electra, too.' The assembly's done.
They're coming: your brother, Pylades, in tears,
Their supporters, weeping and mourning. A sad sight.
Prepare yourself, lady. Knife, noose, you must.
Grand-daughter of Atreus! What use is that to you?

And Apollo, Phoebus Apollo – he's to blame.

The Spanish Golden Age

The three great 17th century playwrights of the golden age in Spanish Drama – Lope de Vega, Calderón de la Barca and Tirso de Molina – wrote hundreds of plays between them (making Shakespeare and his contemporaries look like slow starters!). Though recent revivals may have only scratched the surface of the Spanish Renaissance, the rediscovered plays have revealed a wealth of characters: from obsessive zealous hermits to comic lackeys; lovers in love with the idea of love more than the girl, to fathers more concerned with their own loss of honour than with the violation of their daughters?

The plays generally explore: Religion (the Catholic themes of fate and free will – Tirso de Molina was a monk; Calderón and Lope took minor orders after long, dilettante lives); Love; and, being Mediterranean, Honour. Men choose to be restricted by it, but are slippery with its codes. Women are just restricted by it. Honour is hybrid, synonymous with rank, esteem, pride, status and, most importantly, a woman's chastity: 'How little we value our honour,' tuts a King in Tirso de Molina's *The Last Days of Don Juan*, 'that we leave it in women's care'.

At one and the same time, the plays are poetic, personal, political and deeply conscious of their own theatricality. They are some of the most rewarding roles to be played in the European repertoire.

The Gentleman from Olmedo
(EL CABALLERO DE OLMEDO)

LOPE DE VEGA 1620-1625
translated & adapted by David Johnston 1991

Don Alonso is the *caballero* of the title. He's come from Olmedo to Medina to visit the famous fair. There he falls in love at-first-sight with 'the flower of all Medina', Dona Ines, across the crowds. (Fabia, an old woman, is to deliver a letter from Alonso to Ines.)

ALONSO
Listen, for pity's sake.

As Ines wandered through the fair
her beauty shone before her
like the sun shining through dark night.
Her hair a banner of soft silk
that no ribbon could hold in place;
a banner that called men to war,
a net that trawled us all like fish.
Her gaze was frank and free, and claimed
a life wherever it should rest;
but better to burn in those eyes
than live frozen beyond their spell.
And her hands danced and darted
with the grace of an expert foil,
wounding all the hearts it touched,
hands of living snow she softly
sheathed in her peasant's dull robes
lest each gesture cause a mortal wound.
Her sweet mouth, like a captain's call
recruiting men from all around,
press-ganged an army to her feet.
She wore no coral nor fine pearls
for none could compare to her lips

and teeth; she wore French petticoats,
over them a Basque sea-green skirt,
so that she masked in foreign tongues
the secret of her noble birth.
She walked through the fair, and as she walked
men's souls fell clinging to her heels.
No jasmine flower could be
more beautiful nor more scented.
And as she walked, love ran with her,
bait to the eyes of mortal men,
laughing as like fish we all gaped
and were swiftly netted, though some cried out
and promised her ribbons, silk sashes,
earrings of rich topaz and pearl.
She was deaf to their words. What use
earrings to one who will not hear,
and what use jewels to one whose skin
shines already like finest pearl?
I stopped dead and watched, struck silent,
only my eyes speaking to her,
offering what little I could:
'My soul for a single lock of hair,
my life at your every step'.
And her eyes also spoke to me.
They seemed to plead with me to stay.
'My Alonso of Olmedo,
stay here tonight in Medina.'

So I've placed my trust in those eyes
and have written her this letter
which you will bodly deliver
so that my hopes against all hope
may come true: I would marry her,
my love for her has grown so strong.

(Act I; pp 91-93)

Fuente Ovejuna

LOPE DE VEGA 1612–14
adapted by Adrian Mitchell 1989

Captain Flores reports the Commander's triumphs in battle to rally
the sceptical townspeople of Fuente Ovejuna behind their overlord.

FLORES

I saw it. I was there.
Our mission was to capture Cuidad Real.
The Grand Master assembled his forces:
Two thousand vassals as soldiers on foot.
Three hundred Brothers of the Order
Riding on horseback, red crosses blazing.

Our brave young Master rode out that day
In a green cloak embroidered with gold
Fastened with silken cords over his bright armour.
A magnificent horse, well-fleshed and firm,
A dappled silver-grey like a gale-born cloud,
A steed raised on the clear water of the Betis river
And the deep rich grasses of its meadowbanks,
Its tail was covered by plaited strips
Of cunningly-worked leather, and its mane
Tied in tight curls with whitest ribbons
Which matched the snow-flake marks
Flecking his pale grey flanks.

At his right hand rode Commander Gomez,
Your overlord, upon a sturdy
Stallion the colour of crystallised honey,
With a jet-black mane and tail, but a white underlip.
The Commander wore a cloak
Of flowing, orange-coloured silk
With golden tracery and milky pearls.

His white-plumed helmet seemed to be
Bursting with orange blossom, and he bore
That famous pine tree of a lance
Before which proud Granada trembles.

We advanced, through the dust, towards Cuidad Real.
The city fathers were stubborn.
They took up arms
Shouting "For Ferdinand and Isabella!"
They fought hard, but we beat them down.
Our young Master gave his orders.
Rebel leaders were beheaded.
Their followers were gagged and flogged through the
    streets.
Now the city fears him, the city admires him,
For a youth so suddenly turned conqueror
Will surely grow into a giant
Who will become the scourge of Africa
And overcome a million crescent moons
With his triumphant cross of blood.

He has been generous, too,
Heaping rare gifts upon us,
And he let us plunder the city as freely
As if it were his private property.

But here comes our Commander. Greet him joyfully.
Your smiles and cheers must crown his victory.

(ACT I, SCENE II; PP 42-43)

Fuente Ovejuna

LOPE DE VEGA 1612-14
adapted by Adrian Mitchell 1989

Captain **Flores** reports to the King and Queen that the town of
Fuente Ovejuna has revolted against its (tyrannical) Commander.

The Palace of Ferdinand *and* Isabella.

FLORES

Your majesties. Bad news.
The worst atrocity.

Your majesty, my wounds.
I can't hold out much longer.
They brought me here from Fuente Ovejuna.
The people of that town, the men and the women,
Murdered Commander Gomez.
They worked themselves up
Over nothing at all –
Tore him to shreds, sir.
The whole damned town,
Fuente Ovejuna,
Shouting: Down with the tyrant!
Got so excited by their own shouting
They broke down the doors of his house
And in they burst
And they took no notice when he swore on his honour
To repay anything he owed them,
They took no notice and they struck him down,
Stabbing right through the red cross on his breast
With a thousand vicious gashes,
And they picked him up and sent him flying down
From a high window
And a mob of howling women underneath

Caught his body on the points of pitchforks,
Tossed him, caught him,
Tossed him, dropped him,
Dragged him into a barn.
They fought each other to pull out his hair,
Scratched his face to pieces with their nails.
It was hysteria, your majesties,
So bad that when they'd finished hacking him
The biggest pieces left were his two ears.
They burned his coat of arms.
They sacked his house and looted it.

I was mobbed too,
But managed to find a hiding place.
From there I watched and saw all this.
Later I escaped, was found by your soldiers
And brought here.

Your majesties, punish these barbarians.
The Commander's blood cries out for justice.

(ACT III, SCENE III; PP 85-86)

The Mayor of Zalamea
(EL ALCALDE DE ZALAMEA)

CALDERON 1642
adapted by Adrian Mitchell 1981

Billeted in Zalamea *en route* to Lisbon, the relieved soldiers are
arrogantly looking forward to flirting and bedding the local peasant
women. Their **Captain**, Don Alvaro, has caught sight of the
beautiful Isabel, the daughter of a rich farmer. At dusk, the Captain
loiters longingly round her house with a few of his men. His
Sergeant advises:

> *'Ask yourself: Are you being fair?*
> *You may move on tomorrow, why*
> *Should a young lady hear you out*
> *And come across, all in one day?'.*

(Later the Captain kidnaps Isabel and rapes her in the forest.)

CAPTAIN

All in one day the sun whirls up,
Lights the world, drops into the dark.
All in one day, kingdoms change hands,
Palaces are crushed into dust.
All in one day are cities lost
And gloating victors flood its streets.
All in one day the ocean may
Be level and tumultuous.
All in one day, a man is born.
All in one day, a man must die.
And so, all in one day, my love
May view the darkness and the light
As planets do. All in one day,
My love may rise, my love may fall,
Like an empire. All in one day,
My love may harbour animals,
Like a wood people wander through.

Tame and angry – like the ocean.
Glorious, ruinous – like war.
Love's mastered my passions and mind,
My life and death are in its hand.
And since, all in one day, there's time
To stretch me on the rack like this,
Why's there not time, all in one day,
To bring me home to happiness?
Is there some natural law says:
Love takes longer than injuries?

It takes an instant for a spark
To set a great forest ablaze.
An instant: a volcano roars,
Overflows into an abyss.
An instant: lightning crashes down,
Totally, instantly destroying.
An instant: horror flashes from
The black mouth of the iron cannon.
So why can't love, which after all
Flares up in four distinctive ways –
Fire, volcano, lightning, cannon –
Burn, frighten, wound and devastate?

When a man enters knowingly
A battle area, he goes
Expecting to defend himself
Against a horde of enemies.
But, strolling down a country road,
Far from the war, relaxed, that's when
He runs the greatest risk of all.
The ambush strikes! He's a dead man.

I thought I'd find some bumpkin wench –
I discovered a fine lady.
So obviously I was thrown
Off-balance because unready.
In my whole life I've never seen

A more divine, perfect being.
Her face haunts me:
I'd do anything to see it.

(ACT II; PP 39-40)

The Mayor of Zalamea
(EL ALCALDE DE ZALAMEA)

CALDERON 1642
adapted by Adrian Mitchell 1981

Billeted in Zalamea, the Captain Don Alvaro has become obsessed
with the rich farmer **Crespo's** daughter, Isabel. He kidnaps and rapes
her in the forest. Crespo pursues them but is caught by the Captain's
men and bound to a tree. A distraught Isabel later releases him.

Returning to the town, Crespo is met by a Clerk of the Town
Council who informs him that he has been elected Mayor and
Magistrate: his first case to hear is that of the Captain who has
returned wounded from the forest. 'Justice will be done for you,' he
promises Isabel, 'your father's now the mayor.' He goes to the
Captain and begs him to return his honour – a selfish request – by
marrying his daughter.

CRESPO

Captain, I am an honest man.
I don't boast of my origins
But, God's truth, wouldn't change my state
From peasant to aristocrat.
If titles were my heart's desire
I could afford to buy a crate.
I live among my equals here
And they've always respected me.
The council too has honoured me
And the municipality.
My lands are very wide, well-run
And richer than you could imagine.
In short sir, there is no farmer
Wealthier in this region.

My daughter, sir. She's been brought up

With her late mother's character:
Unselfish, highly virtuous,
Well-spoken of, always sheltered
From poverty and viciousness.
To prove to you her goodness – well
I think that it's enough to say:
Although I'm rich, there's no one who'll
Gossip of me or Isabel –
This, understand, in a small town
Where our sole prevailing fault is
To mull over, not our own
But others' lives and shortcomings
And, God above! We always fail
To agree who's most in the wrong.

My daughter's very beautiful.
Well, you're aware of that or you
Would not have acted as you did.
I wish I didn't have to speak...
I'd weep – and leave the rest unsaid.
Her beauty's my misfortune, sir.
I'll stop, before we swallow down
All of the poison from that cup.
To test our strength – let some remain.
What's happened must be made to look
Less like a monstrosity.
What's happened is so mountainous
It can't be covered up at all
Or God knows I would bury it
In the grave of my mourning soul.
And then I would not come to you
Or argue like this, for you see
What's happened would then only be
A secret tearing inside me.
The sickness is so evident –
Some cure must be open to me.
      kill you? Honour remains sick –
         revenge, not a remedy.

I've looked at it from every side
And I can only see one way
I'd accept and you might accept,
This: you take all my property –
My house, my money and my land.
Neither my son nor I will keep
A penny, we'll be beggarmen.
And, if you wish, brand both of us
With red-hot irons, and in chains
Stand us upon the auction block
And sell us for obedient slaves,
And thus you'll raise a further sum
Beyond the dowry of your bride.

Give me my reputation back.
I believe you won't be dishonoured.
Sir, you'll have sons, and all the shame
Of being grandchildren of mine
Will be erased, for they will live
As sons of yours, as noblemen.
As the Castilian proverb says:
"The stallion makes up for the mare."

(kneels)

Look, on my knees I beg you now,
By these tears and these grey hairs.
What am I begging for? I beg
For honour. Give it back to me.
Although it's mine, it seems to be
Something of yours, because I plead
For it with such humility.
You know that I am empowered
To take. But I want to give.

(ACT III; PP 74-76)

Life's a Dream
(LA VIDA ES SUEÑO)

CALDERON 1635
adapted by Adrian Mitchell & John Barton 1983

The King of Poland incarcerated his son **Sigismund,** at birth, in the
craggy rocks of a ravine, far removed from society – though not from
a simple education. The learned King had predicted terrifying omens
from the stars about his son's life – the first of which came true when
Sigismund's mother died as he was born:

> 'I knew then that he would grow up to be vicious.
> A cruel prince and a despotic King;
> That Poland would be torn by civil war
> And that his wildness would debauch the Kingdom
> Into a foul academy of chaos ... I decided
> That I must cage the beast and find out whether
> One cunning King could overcome the stars'.

Sigismund *comes forward, chained. He is carrying a picture-book.*

SIGISMUND

What have I done that I should suffer so?
What crime has been committed? Tell me, stars.
I have been born. Is that a crime in men?
Were other men not born as I was born?
Yet they are blessed and I have here no blessings.

(turns over the pages of the book)

A bird is born, a swallow,
Little and damp and shaken,
It grows so bright and dark and feathery,
A spray of flowers on the wing.
It slices through the air so speedily
That it outflies imagining

And leaves its nest forsaken.
Then why can't I
Be like a swallow flying free?

(he turns the page to a picture of a salmon)

A fish is born, a salmon.
Child of the waterfall's rock and sprays.
Its rainbow armour fitting perfectly,
It cuts the oceans like a knife,
Charting and measuring the sea
And all the million forms of life
In the vast cold waterways.
Then why can't I
Be like a salmon swimming free?

(he turns the page to a picture of a waterfall)

A spring is born, a stream,
Welling up among grass to go
As serpents travel, swift and windingly.
The river sings its silver thanks
And joys in its mobility
To flowers and beasts along its banks
As they watch its dazzling flow.
Then why can't I
Be like a river, flowing free?

(he turns to a picture of a leopard)

A beast is born, a leopard,
Delicate as a hyacinth.
Its shaven hide is dappled cunningly
With paintbrush marks of black and gold.
But the grown leopard shows a cruelty
That's natural, so we are told,
A monster in a labyrinth.
Then why, why, can't I

Be like a leopard running free?

Born out of rage,
Eaten with rage,
I'm a volcano. Watch me bleed.
Give me a knife – I'll show you surgery
And wrench out, raggedy and raw
Bits of my heart. Captivity!
So is there some reason or some law
Denies me the one thing I need,
Which God gave swallows and salmon too,
And beasts and leopards: to be free?

(ACT I, SCENE I; PP 95-96)

Life's a Dream
(LA VIDA ES SUEÑO)

CALDERON 1635
adapted by Adrian Mitchell & John Barton 1983

Sigismund, the son of the King of Poland, has been imprisoned in the mountains since birth, far away from society, because of terrible omens his father had read into the stars. The King, testing and challenging celestial signs, decides to bring Sigismund to his palace, where Sigismund sees, hears and feels things he has only ever read about. His over-excitement leads, unfortunately, to him attacking a woman, fighting a prince, and throwing a servant into a lake. The King regards this as proof that he cannot dictate fate, that his son is evil; so he sedates Sigismund and throws him back in prison. Sigismund awakes and wonders whether his experiences have all been a dream.

SIGISMUND

In this strange world to live's a kind of dreaming,
And each of us must dream the thing he is
Till he awakes. The King dreams he's a King,
Lives, orders, governs in a royal illusion,
Because his fame is written in the wind.
For every King that rules men in his King-dream
Must wake at last in the cold sleep of death.
The rich man dreams his riches which are cares,
The poor man dreams his penury and pain,
The man who prospers dreams, the man who strives,
The man who hurts men, and the man who's hurt,
All dream. So what's this life? A fraud, a frenzy,
A trick, a tale, a shadow, an illusion.
And all our life is nothing but a dream.
And what are dreams? They are no more than dreamstuff.
And what is real is nothing, and a man
Is nothing neither. It is all a dream.

(ACT II, SCENE II; P 138)

Damned for Despair
(EL CONDENADO POR DESCONFIADO)

TIRSO DE MOLINA 1620
adapted & translated by Laurence Boswell 1991

Paulo, a zealous hermit, lives in a cave in the mountain forests
beyond Naples. He leads a life of poverty, piety and intense prayer.
Untempted by the Devil for ten years, Paulo's faith is finally shaken.

Enter Paulo *in great distress*.

PAULO
I'm defeated by a dream!
Death came to my cave,
And drove me from prayer,
The dream told a story
Which burns into my soul.
Have I offended God or
Is this the Devil's dream?

As I knelt in meditation
Death danced about me
Swinging her scythe through me
Without breaking my flesh.
Oh God in heaven help me,
Then she lay down her scythe
And loaded the arrow
Which ends all human courage,
Her right hand gripped the bow
Then she shot right through my heart.
I watched my chest split,
Watched drops of blood sink
And saw my body falling
Like a beast in the slaughter.
Then my soul flew away
And I saw the face of God,

The face I'd lived to see,
Oh, it was hard and cold,
Brutal and unmoving.
In His hand he held a sword,
At his side was the Devil,
Smiling at a victory,
For he had won my soul.
Satan read out my sins,
Whilst Michael, who guards the
Newly dead, spoke of my
Good deeds; in the scales
My life was weighed, the left
Scale came down fast while
The right leapt up and so
God pointed down to Hell,
And my soul began to fall
To the place of terror.
I woke up from my dream,
Shaking on the cave floor,
In a pool of freezing sweat,
With the smell of rotting
Flesh burning in my nose.

What does this dream mean?
Does it predict my fate
Or is it Satan's trickery?
O merciful God above
Please help me understand,
Am I condemned to Hell
Or will I die and live
Again with You: in the
Paradise of Your love,
I've walked the narrow path;
Surely I'll go to Heaven,
Please God, end my doubt,
Will I go to Heaven,
Or must I go Hell?

(ACT I SCENE III; PP 14-15)

Damned for Despair
(EL CONDENADO POR DESCONFIADO)

TIRSO DE MOLINA 1620
adapted & translated by Laurence Boswell 1991

Disguised as an angel, the Devil has made the pious hermit Paulo believe that his fate is inextricably linked to a Neopolitan called **Enrico,** son of Anareto. Sent to The Gate of the Sea by the Devil-angel, Paulo observes Enrico's gang at a picnic where Enrico sets up the challenge:

'I want us all to tell
The story of our lives.
The man whose story
Tells of most wickedness,
Evil and depravity,
Will win a crown of roses,
Have songs written for him,
And sung to him whilst
Bottles of wine are
Poured down his throat'.

ENRICO

I was born to be evil,
As my story will reveal.

I grew up here in Naples,
Son of a rich merchant,
You all know my old father,
He was born a commoner,
He earned the title rich man,
Which has always seemed to me
The most useful decoration.
As a child I stole
My father's hard-won fortune,
I stole coins from his purse
And later sold the purses.

I discovered the secret places
Where he kept his money and
I stole it all, every penny.
Then I made my first friends,
The dice, the card table and
The wheel: gambling became
My life, and gambling
Is the father of all crime.
I quickly lost the money
I'd stolen from my father,
So I turned to burglary.
I broke into people's homes,
Taking anything of value,
And went straight back to the dice,
The card table and the wheel,
Where I lost the money
I'd made from my robberies.

So then I joined a gang
Of specialist thieves who
Shared my love of gambling.
We did about fifty homes,
Killing six men in the process.
We worked as a team,
Dividing everything equally
We made together, and
We all went straight back to the
Dice, the cards, and the wheel.
One night the police chased us,
They caught everyone but me,
And despite being tortured,
No one gave my name.
As I watched them in the square,
Each one swinging on a rope,
I decided to work alone.
I learnt to stand outside
The gambling house at night,
Waiting for the winners,

From whom I begged. And, as they
Reached into their pockets,
I reached for my dagger
And buried it deeply
Between their unsuspecting ribs.
So, what they'd quickly won inside
They quickly lost again to me.

I started mugging women,
They're easier to overcome;
I threatened them with a blade,
And if they didn't yield,
I'd slash their lovely faces.

That's how I spent my youth;
Now I'll tell you of the man.

For all my adult life,
This sword's been my best friend,
Between us we've stopped the lives
Of thirty unlucky souls.
Ten I killed for nothing,
I mean I didn't get paid.
I killed the rest for money.
I've killed for one gold coin,
Which might sound a little cheap,
But I swear before you all,
When I'm short of money,
I'll kill for the price of
A drink, or a game of cards.

I've raped six poor virgins,
Which is lucky I suppose,
It's hard to meet one virgin,
In these dark, sad times.

I wasn't so lucky one night,
When I broke into a house,

To make love to a woman
Who was married to a banker.
She woke up in her bed and
Screamed, I wasn't invited.
Her husband appeared waving
A sword and shouting insults.
I punched him in the face, picked
Him up by his grey hair
And threw him off the balcony,
Which was three floors up.
The bitch got hysterical,
So I razored her breasts,
Five times, or maybe six.
As rivers of blood flooded
The meadow of her belly,
I watched her soul fly away.

Once I was organising
Protection for some people
Who owned little shops.
One of the businessmen
Refused to pay his dues,
So I had to go after him,
He took refuge in a school,
The teachers locked the doors
So I couldn't get at him.
I set fire to the place and
Everyone was burned to death.
All the children turned to ash.

I enjoy offending God,
I've never been to Mass,
Never confessed my sins.
I hate the poor and needy,
I've watched men die of hunger,
While my purse was full of gold.
I've no fear of the law,
I've killed so many policemen,

They've stopped trying to arrest me.
I'm beyond their jurisdiction.

My final and worst crime
Is that I love this woman.
Her eyes are the only jail
Which can hold me prisoner.
But when I'm short of money,
I take all her earnings,
And leave her with nothing.
I take her money, and go
To see my father, you all
Know old Anareto.
He lives alone in poverty,
For five years he's suffered
Some incurable affliction,
He's crippled, he can hardly walk.
He sits at home waiting for
Me to turn up with some food.
I blame myself for his ills,
He's never recovered from
Losing all his money to the
Dice, the cards and the wheel.

Everything I've said is true,
I swear by Jesus Christ.
So, judges, what's the verdict?
Who deserves the prize?

(ACT I, SCENE XIII; PP 36-40)

Damned for Despair
(EL CONDENADO POR DESCONFIADO)

TIRSO DE MOLINA 1620
adapted & translated by Laurence Boswell 1991

In the mountain forests beyond Naples, the hermit Paulo lives in a cave adjacent to his protegé: the less pious **Pedrisco**.

Enter Pedrisco. He carries a very large bundle of grass, twigs, and other vegetation.

PEDRISCO

Enter me, with donkey food,
Grasses, twigs and shrubbery,
If I eat all this greenery,
I see an awful end for me,
And it won't be constipation.

God did You create me
To eat the food You made,
For donkeys, cows and grubs?
If You did, then send me
The patience: not to
Mention the digestion,
To endure such a fate.

It's all my mother's fault!
When I fell into the world
From between her fat thighs,
She said, Oh my baby,
You've the eyes of a saint.
So that's what I'm supposed
To be, thank God I never
Married, think what a
Mother-in-law might suggest.

Good Lord, I understand
Sainthood is an honour but
Hunger's a strange blessing.
Forgive me this frailty, Lord,
Forgive my weak belly.
Now, as I've confessed my sins,
Could I call on Your mercy
And make a small suggestion.
If you remove my yearnings,
I'll be a better hermit,
Sainthood would be easy.
Oh Lord, another request:
Could I beg a dispensation
To forget about fasting.
I like to eat big dinners,
And fat people need a saint.

Ten years ago I left home,
And came here with Paulo,
He lives in that cave and
This is my hermitage.
Here we do our penance,
Eating grass, twigs, and shrubs.
I'm sad when I think of the
Plenty I've left behind,
And the nothing I have here.

Sometimes as the waterfall
Splashes out a sad tune,
I sing a lament to
Some old friends in Naples:
"Oh pigs of my back yard
Take pity on your master,
You pigs of my back yard,
Oh where are you now?"
When I walked down stone streets
And not over rocks and roots,
You were so sensitive

To every rumble of
My big hungry belly.
Oh you were so loyal,
Giving bacon, chops and ham
Now I never see a snout.

Well, hunger's beaten me again,
I'll have to go and eat,
As I say grace over
This grassy feast, I'll beg
Heaven for protection,
Because after such a meal,
My belly swells so much
That I think I'm pregnant and
Sometimes I'm terrified
That I might give birth
To a whole flock of sheep.
And sometimes I imagine I
Might give birth to the Spring,
I've eaten so many seeds.

(ACT I, SCENE II; PP 12-14)

The Last Days of Don Juan
(El Burlador de Sevilla y Convidado de Piedra)

Tirso de Molina 1616-1625
adapted by Nick Dear 1990

Don Juan's scrapes with women – such as deflowering Isabella in
Naples, disguised as her fiancé – have forced him to return to Seville.
There he bumps into his old mate the Marquis of Mota. Mota tells
him about 'Nature's finest creation', Dona Anna, who has been
promised to another, despite Mota's adoration. While Mota goes to
find out more about Anna's fate, and Don Juan is left alone, Anna
appears at a barred window and entrusts the stranger with a letter to
her forbidden lover.

DON JUAN

Well! What kind of chimera was that? Was it real? Or an
illusion? A letter, dropped into my hands like a formal
invitation from heaven. For sure, that was the girl the
Marquis of Mota has fallen for. You can see why, too. In
Seville I am called a seducer and a rogue, and frankly, with
good reason – my great pleasure's to hunt down women
and abuse them, and leave them weeping hot tears for their
honour. This little one I'll tear open, as soon as I've left the
square. But wait – the seal is still wet. *(laughs)* A skilful
intrigue, this. It's signed by Dona Anna, in a round,
cultured hand.

"My darling, my brute father has arranged my nuptial mass.
I cannot disobey. And yet I cannot live without you. If you
love me as keenly as you say, as I so dearly love you, too,
(come to the courtyard door tonight at eleven o'clock; the
maid will let you in. Wear your crimson cloak so she knows
you. And cousin, be true, as I am true to you, too, for ever.
Your unhappy love —"

(laughs) Oh dear, oh dear. Stupid girl. I'll take her as I took old Isabella, in the marble halls of Naples...

(ACT I, SCENE VI; P 35)

The Last Days of Don Juan
(EL BURLADOR DE SEVILLA Y CONVIDADO DE PIEDRA)

TIRSO DE MOLINA 1616–1625
adapted by Nick Dear 1990

Don Gonzalo has just returned to Seville from his ambassadorial
mission to Lisbon. After reporting the diplomatic success, he is asked
by the King to tell him about Lisbon: 'What's it like? Nice place?'.
After Don Gonzalo's description, the King replies: 'Your brief
account brings Lisbon to life with such colour, such vigour, that
listening to your description is, I'm sure, preferable to actually going
there'.

DON GONZALO
Lisbon is the eighth wonder of the world!

In the bowels of Spain, in the province of Cuenca,
The mighty River Tagus has its source.
From there it tears our countryside in two,
Flowing swiftly to the sea, streaming lastly
Through the heart of ancient Lisbon.
At the mouth it forms a port
Between two high sierras; here you may see
Ships of all the navies of the world!
Barques, caravels, galleons rigged for war,
Scarred veterans of our American conquests –
All guarded on the westward side, where lies
The vast Atlantic, by two enormous fortresses,
Cascais and St John.

Half a league outside the city, at Belem, you find
The monastery of St Jerome, containing
The tombs of all the Kings and Queens of Portugal,
And Vasco da Gama, navigator of the globe.
From here the city appears

Like a cluster of jewels, dangled from the sky...

The beautiful streets unfold with convents,
Churches and ancestral homes, where noblemen,
Scholars and soldiers live, upholding their
Great laws. But the finest building of all
Is the Misericordia, pride of the city,
And envy of Spain.
From the high towers of this colossal structure
You see no less than sixty towns
Along the sunny coast. Lisbon is ringed
By twelve hundred estates.
The land is fertile, the people content.
The roads are lined with poplar trees.
The orchards drip with nuts and fruit.

Precisely at the centre of the city is the Rossio,
A handsome square, which but a hundred years ago
Was covered by the sea. But the sea,
Succumbing to the pull of some strange tide,
Flowed on, and thirty thousand houses now stand
Proudly in its place.
There is a street called 'Rua Nova' –
'New Street' to you and me –
Full of oriental treasure, where the merchants
Count their money by the sack-full! – according
To the King. He lives in a magnificent residence
Called Terrero. Here is moored an armada from
France, England, the North,
With cargoes of barley and wheat. Wrought in iron
In the gates is the royal coat of arms:
A red sphere at its base to symbolise
The bloody wounds suffered by Alonso Enriquez
In his first crusade for Christ against the Moor.

Most impressive.

In Lisbon you can sit eating supper,

Drinking the sparkling wine,
With the fishermens' nets so close it seems
Your food has vaulted straight from sea to table!
Every night a thousand ships arrive
With rare, exotic goods,
Oils and spices, meat and grain,
Every kind of fruit, and ice
From the hills of Estrella
Which the women sell from baskets on their heads!

But I must end.

To try and mention every detail
Of this glorious location
Would be to try and count the stars
That fill the sky. Let it suffice
That there are living there
One hundred and thirty thousand
Of your loyal Christian subjects,
And a solitary King, who through myself
Would kiss your hand.

(ACT I, SCENE IV; PP 22-24)

Don Gil of the Green Breeches
(DON GIL DE LAS CALZAS VERDES)

TIRSO DE MOLINA 1611
adapted & translated by Laurence Boswell 1990

Dona Juana, disguised as a man (Don Gil), has arrived in Madrid in pursuit of her unfaithful lover. To complete the trappings of an honourable Don, Dona Juana/Don Gil needs a lackey. S/he stumbles across **Caramanchel** as he's turfed out of his lodgings for not paying his bills. 'Hello,' s/he says,

> *'I was just*
> *Enquiring if you were*
> *Looking for a master?'.*

CARAMANCHEL
        If the heavens
Were to rain down masters,
Or if every insect
Changed into a master,
Or if masters went around
Crying out for lackeys,
Or the streets of Madrid
Were all paved with masters,
I still wouldn't find one;
I'm unlucky, you see,
When it comes to masters.

I've suffered many,
Loads, and every one of them
A nightmare: I served
A doctor once, big beard,
Thick lips, but he wasn't
German; smart suits, velvet shoes,
Lemon silk accessories,
Lots of books but no cures.

After his surgery
He would always reserve
A medicinal draft
For himself: olives, stews,
Sides of ham and chicory;
He was never tempted to
Stuff himself with knowledge:
All the patients got were
Leeches and stale pots of pee.

He had a curious way
Of making diagnoses:
"Your malady, my lady,
Is a touch of wind and
Hypochondria", and then
He'd unbutton her dress
To feel congestion on her chest.

I never suffered the curse
Of a heavy pocket
In his employment, for
In matters of wages
His conscience weighed upon
Him extremely lightly.
It would be fair to say
When it came to money
His memory was as good
As his skill in curing
Anyone of anything.

After that I worked for
A narcissistic barrister
Who'd only take on cases
Which could earn him easy cash.
It made me so angry to
See his waiting room full
Of poor anxious plaintiffs

While he lounged in his office
Combing his greasy hair
And waxing his moustache.

Next I waited
On a pot-bellied priest
Who wouldn't say a word
To save a starving sinner
But was very eloquent
When thinking of his dinner.
"Ah how good is the Lord",
He'd sigh with eyes to heaven
And hands on well fed stomach,
"Now tell me, Caramanchel,
What Holy man only called
God good when he had dined?"
He expected his staff
To observe every fast day
While he made himself fat.
It was blind hypocrisy!
I bawled him out; that was that.

Six lean months I skivvied
For a penniless knight
Who spent his time dreaming
Of a worthy cause to fight.
Most weeks it dawned on him
A lackey needed payment,
But when money got tight
He forgot our arrangement.
I thought it quite unfair
That I had to go hungry;
I'm not sure if he noticed
Or simply didn't care.
He had a novel way
Of saying the Lord's Prayer:
"Give me this day your daily
Bread", and of course Caramanchel did.

So sadly I was forced
Into embezzlement:
His poor horse subsisted
On half a peck of straw a week
Which I peddled on the side;
So I saw off starvation
But the horse nearly died.
I couldn't live like that.

Then I went to work for
A certain Lord Elderly
Who'd married a very young lady
Near the end of his life;
The peculiarity
Of our contract was that
He expected me to serve him
While servicing his wife.

If I was to tell you
About all the bizarre
Masters I've ever had,
And I've had more than there
Are blisters on a leper,
You'd be asleep before
I got half way down the list.

No, I'm unemployed
Because I am honest.

(ACT I, SCENE II; PP 111-114)

The Seventeenth Century

17th century French drama established classical codes of comedy and tragedy which subsequently permeated the whole of European theatre. Though the names of Molière (comedy) and Racine (tragedy) are the most well-known to us, it was Corneille (comedy *and* tragedy) who established the parameters of both classical genres. His boisterous comedies sparkle with wit; his sincere tragedies elegantly, yet passionately examine the conflicts between private love and public duty.

Dryden, in England's Restoration, was the first of many commentators to shy away from French tragedy as untranslatable because of its rhyming couplets – English tragedians have always been more fond of blank verse. Where zestful rhyme appeals in comedy, it might not always be assumed to be appropriate for tragedy by English-speaking performers. Thus Noel Clark's tragic couplets in his Corneille translations and Neil Bartlett's in Racine's *Bérénice* are as considerable an achievement and challenge to the perfomer as Bartlett's and Ranjit Bolt's dazzling rhymes in Molière's comedies.

Bartlett writes his Molière and Racine translations phonetically so that you can see how they scan (so 'prare' is one syllable where 'prayer' would be two). Of this twelve syllable form he says: 'I want the audience to be aware at all times that these texts are a mapping of modern language and modern theatre over the language and theatre of another time and place. I want them to sound both English and foreign'.

Noel Clark is also the translator of the Dutch/Flemish writer Joost van den Vondel. Clark replaces Vondel's rhyming Alexandrines with rhyming pentameters, making this unfamiliar work more accessible. *Lucifer* was written in 1654, thirteen years before Milton's epic poem *Paradise Lost* presented its own dynamic portrait of a Lucifer at odds with God. Like the French tragedians, Vondel explores the struggle between obedience and free will. Holland in the 17th century was a volatile patchwork of religious protest and political turmoil. Vondel himself converted to Catholicism in 1641, which cost him some of the critical popularity he had enjoyed hitherto. *Lucifer* was banned after two performances by the zealous Calvinist authorities: 'Though the action is set in Heaven, Vondel's celestial beings are all too human in their frailty,' notes Clark wryly. Vondel wasn't a frail man, writing *Lucifer* in his 60s and living to the age of 91 (1587-1679)! The cultural zenith of the Dutch/Flemish Golden Age – usually associated with the painters Rembrandt, Van Dyke and Rubens – owes much to his drama.

Lucifer

JOOST VAN DEN VONDEL 1654
translated & adapted by Noel Clark 1988

Raphael, one of the seven Archangels, has been sent by God with
an olive branch to disperse the rebel angels peacefully. Led by
Lucifer, they are revolting against God's preference for Man which
challenges their power in Heaven. Raphael is there in 'anguish but
good will', pleading with Lucifer to lay down his arms.

RAPHAEL
For pity's sake! Wherefore in war-attire
Should you confront me? I am sore distraught
With grief on your account! Medicine I've brought –
The salve of Holy Grace, freely provided
By God who, with His Counsellors, decided
You to anoint – above a thousand peers –
As His crowned Deputy in all the spheres.
What lunacy has so confused your mind?
You, on whose holy brow the Godhead signed
His likeness and His seal, on you bestowing
Beauty and wisdom, favours ever-flowing
From His great treasure-fount in copious streams?
Next God in Paradise, you cast your beams,
As from a cloud of dew and roses fresh;
Your festive raiment was a solid mesh
Of pearls and rubies, emeralds, gold-encrusted;
The heaviest sceptre to your hand was trusted;
When you appeared, trumpets and drums resounded –
The echoes from the very stars rebounded!
You'd recklessly reject such pomp and pride –
Beauty and splendour lightly cast aside?
Your radiance which adds to Heaven's lustre,
Eclipsing ours, you'd hazard for a cluster
Of beasts and crude monstrosities instead:
A griffon's razor-claws, a dragon's head?

These horrors you'd prefer to put on show?
That Heaven's stars should see you brought so low!
For oath betrayed, all power and glory gone!
May God forbid, whose face I gaze upon
In light perpetual, as we Blessed Seven,
Trembling, wait upon the Throne of Heaven –
Before that Majesty that gilds our brows
And every living thing with life endows!
Lord Deputy, I pray you, do not spurn
My plea. My aim is pure and my concern
Heartfelt! Put off your armour, doff your crest,
Fling down your shield and war-axe lay to rest!
No longer strive! Surrender, I implore!
Lower your standard, fold your wings before
The Godhead's glittering omnipotence,
Lest from this pinnacle He cast you hence,
And grind you all to powder for your pains,
So that no trace of Angelkind remains:
No root nor branch, no memory of life –
Not even one of misery and strife –
Of death, despair, remorse, eternal shame
And gnashing teeth – unworthy of life's name!
Here, seize this olive-branch! Capitulate!
Accept God's mercy now – else it's too late!

(ACT IV; PP 51-52)

Lucifer

JOOST VAN DEN VONDEL 1654
translated & adapted by Noel Clark 1988

Lucifer was God's favoured angel – 'His crowned Deputy in all the
spheres' – but he has formed an army of angels to rebel against God's
decision which places Man above angels. Lucifer's fury makes him
reject the olive branch offered by Raphael, God's envoy. Even
though he knows God's might to be almighty, Lucifer believes he
has no choice but to pursue the fight, having gone too far to
withdraw.

LUCIFER

So wretchedly, did creature ever veer
Between faint hope and overwhelming fear?
If victory's doubtful, is defeat in store
For him who with the Godhead hazards war?
Who, for the first time ever, takes a stand
Against God's Holy Will and high command,
Leads insurrection 'gainst the Godhead's Throne
To change the laws of Heaven for his own –
Bearing the curse of base ingratitude,
Spurning the love, grace and beatitude
Of bounteous Father, source of all that we've
Been blest with in the past, or shall receive?
My steps have strayed too far from duty's path!
I have abjured my Maker, scorned His wrath!
How can my blasphemous arrogance be concealed?
There's no way back! I've climbed too high to yield!
What shall I do? How act in my despair?
Time brooks no pause. Had I a minute spare,
That were not time enough – if time at all –
The instant twixt Salvation and the Fall!
Too late! No cure for blemish so profound!
All hope is lost. I hear God's trumpet sound!

(ACT IV; PP 55–56)

The Liar
(LE MENTEUR)

PIERRE CORNEILLE 1643
translated & adapted by Ranjit Bolt 1989

Dorante is a compulsive liar, who embellishes everything, making it
up as he goes along. Having left university, he has just arrived in
Paris full of *joie de vivre*. His father has found him a suitable fiancée.
But Dorante has his own plans and invents an elaborate story to foil
his father.

DORANTE

Very soon after my arrival there
I met Orphise. Her charms, beyond compare,
Would have subdued a heart of flint. Her gaze
Transfixed me with its bright, soul-searching rays.
I sought an introduction: the reward
For my attentions was her kind regard;
Within six months she had returned my love
With secret favours ... nothing to reprove
Until at last I had obtained the right
To climb into her bedroom, late at night. ...
Just for a chat. One night – I can remember
The date – it was the second of November –
(It was the night that I was caught, you see)
Her father had been dining out, and we
Heard him come up the stairs, and stop, and knock
On the bedroom door. Orphise got quite a shock!
She froze, then blenched, then blushed, then used her head –
She drew the curtains round me in the bed,
And let him in. She seemed to have a plan:
She hugged him – almost choked the poor old man –
So that it wouldn't look as though he'd caught her
Off guard. He took a seat, and told his daughter
He'd just received a very handsome offer

For her hand! Picture what I had to suffer.
She managed to respond so cleverly
As to please him, without alarming me.
At length they finished this distressing chat –
But just as he was going out – guess what?
My watch began to strike! He dropped the latch,
And said: "I didn't know you had a watch.
Who gave it you?" "Cousin Acaste," she stalled,
"Just brought it round – he wants it overhauled.
It seems to go off every other minute.
His quarter's got no decent jewellers in it."
"Give it to me. That's easily corrected,"
He said. Orphise came over to collect it   –
I passed it through the curtains, but in vain –
My pistol got entangled with the chain,
Which pulled the trigger and discharged a shot.
Disaster! Orphise fainted on the spot.
Her father hurled himself onto the floor,
And shouted *"Assassins!"* and *"Au secours!"*
His son and several servants blocked my path,
But I was practically insane with wrath:
I drew my sword and tried to force my way
Between them, but, in the ensuing fray,
My rapier snapped, which forced me to give ground.
Meanwhile, Orphise was starting to come round:
Recent events had clearly stunned her, but
She was sufficiently alert to shut
The bedroom door, with only her and me
Inside. We both began, spontaneously,
To pile up boxes, tables, chairs and beds,
In a huge barricade; we'd lost our heads –
As if our puny efforts could achieve
Anything better than a brief reprieve!
They smashed a hole and entered through the wall –
I saw the game was up, and had to call
Our struggle to a halt.
I'd compromised the girl – what could I do?

Found in her bedroom, and at midnight, too!
I had to marry her to save her honour,
In view of the apparent wrong I'd done her.
What's more, I was outnumbered five to one –
Now tell me, father, what would you have done?
Besides, the ordeal that we'd just been through
Together made me feel her charms anew.
And so, in one fell swoop, I saved my life,
Salvaged a girl's good name and gained a wife.

(ACT II; PP 30–31)

The Illusion
(L'ILLUSION COMIQUE)

PIERRE CORNEILLE 1635
translated & adapted by Ranjit Bolt 1989

Matamore is a self-important knight devoted to his lady Isabelle. He
has a vivid imagination and brags of his knightly pursuits to his
servant Clindor. He's a softy, all swashbuckling mouth but puny
muscle.

MATAMORE

The very mention of my name can make
Ramparts collapse and massed batallions quake;
In fact, I'd barely need to rouse myself
To strip those princes of their power and wealth –
I'd only have to blow ... My breath
Is capabale of scattering instant death!
The thunder is my cannon, Destiny
My standard-bearer, and you talk to me
Of armies! *(quite suddenly, he becomes calm)*
    Ah! A sudden, amorous thought
Has swooped on me, and made my mind its sport!
Her image causes anger to subside
And drives away all thoughts of homicide!
Her whim disposes of my liberty –
Cupid, who governs all, must govern me!
Witness the transformation in my face,
As bestial rage gives way to manly grace!

I can be anything I choose to be:
A wolf, a lamb, it's all the same to me –
As whim dicates, I'll tear a man apart
Or melt some unsuspecting woman's heart.
I had to cultivate my brutal side
To stop the ladies pestering me – they tried

To touch me everywhere I went – as soon
As I appeared they'd go beserk, or swoon!
Life was impossible – queens and princesses
Held to ransom for my own caresses;
In short, from Ethiopia to Japan,
I was the archetypal ladies' man;
In Turkey several beauties, hoping to...
Liaise with me, left the Seraglio
And got me into trouble with the Sultan.

But these activities distracted me
From wars of conquest, and eventually,
Exhausted, I instructed Destiny
To visit heaven and demand of Jove
Some respite from this unremitting love;
I strengthened my petition with a threat
To oust the mighty Thunderer from his seat
And give his bolts to Mars. In mortal, or
Rather, immortal fear, Heaven's governor
Granted my suit. Since then, as you can see,
I'm only handsome when I choose to be!

Goddesses have succumbed to me as well.
They have! There are some stories I could tell...

(ACT II; PP 81-83)

Le Cid

PIERRE CORNEILLE 1637
translated by Noel Clark 1993

Rodrigo is the King's loyal champion, hero of the battle against the Moors. He acted on his own initiative and is reporting the victory to the King.

RODRIGO

Led by me, our troop at once
Set out with manly show of confidence –
Five hundred strong – and rallied swift support.
We were three thousand when we reached the port.
At sight of us with our determined faces,
Even the faint-hearts longed to show their paces.
Two thirds of them I hid, well out of sight,
On vessels in the harbour overnight;
The rest of them, with me – their numbers growing –
Impatience to do battle clearly showing –
I bade lie down and wait without a sound;
Much of the night we spent upon the ground.
The sentries likewise hid, by my command,
Thus helping execute the ruse I planned.
To make quite sure my orders were obeyed,
I claimed they came from you, Sire, I'm afraid!
By starlight's pallid gleam at last we saw
The sails of thirty Moorish men-o-war;
The tide incoming bore them on its breast;
Thus, into harbour, ships and sea progressed.
We let them pass and gave no sign at all:
No guards patrolled the port nor city wall.
The silence doubtless led them to surmise
They'd taken us completely by surprise.
They anchored inshore – fearless, made to land
And found themselves beset on every hand.

We all sprang up and shouted to the skies,
Shattering the silence with a thousand cries,
While those we'd hid in vessels, joined the chorus,
And burst forth armed. In disarray before us,
The Moors, still disembarking – seized with fright –
Lost heart before they had a chance to fight.
They'd come to pillage, but were met with war;
We savaged them afloat, no less ashore.
Their blood was streaming ere the Moorish troop
Had time to mount resistance or regroup.
But all too soon, their princes stemmed the rout.
The Moors, with newfound courage, turned about:
The shame of death before they'd struck a blow
Sufficed to close their ranks and, hearts aglow,
They stood their ground and drew their scimitars;
Mixing their blood horrendously with ours!
The shore, the river, galleons and port
Were killing grounds where death alone made sport!
How many gallant exploits, out of sight,
Were robbed of glory, shrouded by the night.
Since only he who struck his blow could see,
None could predict defeat or victory!
I moved about, encouraging our brothers,
Bidding some race ahead, supporting others,
Disposing new arrivals in their turn.
Not until dawn could I myself discern
How far the odds had mounted in our favour;
The Moors, perceiving this, began to waver:
Fresh reinforcements on our flanks descrying,
Their will to win gave way to fear of dying.
Retreating to their ships, they cut the ropes,
With dreadful cries, abandoning their hopes,
Nor, terrified, did any stop to see
Whether their potentates could also flee.
Their terror was too great for such concern:
The tide that brought them, took them on the turn.
Meanwhile, their kings gave fight although surrounded,
With one or two supporters gravely wounded,

Determined that their lives should cost us dear.
I called on them to yield; they wouldn't hear
But scimitar in hand, fought bravely on
Till those few knights had perished, whereupon
The kings, perceiving their resistance vain,
Surrendered and acknowledged me their thane.
I sent them both to you, Sire, as of right:
So battle ceased, with no one left to fight!

(ACT IV, SCENE II; PP 59-61)

Cinna

Pierre Corneille 1640
translated by Noel Clark 1992

Cinna conspires to murder Augustus, the Emperor of Rome, on
behalf of his love, Emilia, who is seeking vengeance for Augustus'
murder of her own father. Emilia says she will marry Cinna once he
has done this deed. Yet Augustus trusts Cinna as his confidant, asking
him how (or if) to rule. As a reward for his advice, he offers Cinna
the hand of Emilia in marriage. Cinna is in a moral dilemma.

CINNA

Weakness? No, it deserves a nobler name –
This virtuous sentiment ... For where's the shame,
In honour's cause, rash actions to preclude,
Born of cowardice and ingratitude?
But maybe call it weakness after all,
Since it cannot withstand a lover's thrall:
A love respecting, which it should suppress
Afraid resistance might achieve success!
In this dilemma, what should I decide?
Which way to turn? By whose advice abide?
It's shame for man of honour to defect!
Regardless of the fruits I might expect –
The sweets of love, revenge's worthy prize,
The freedom of my land – none, in my eyes,
Is so alluring as to capture me,
If I'm required to stoop to treachery:
To stab a prince, so gracious as to deem
My humble self worth his august esteem,
Who's honoured me with wealth and fame and who'll
Take only my advice on how to rule.
No! Treason is unworthy of a man!
Let Rome's enslavement untold ages span –
Perish my love and all my hopes expire –

Rather than I commit a crime so dire!
Already, he's offered me all I want in life:
Why should I spill his blood to buy my wife?
Can't I enjoy his gifts, while still he lives?
Why seize by force what he so freely gives?
Thanks to that reckless oath, I am not free –
Emilia's hate, her father's memory!
My word, heart, hand – my all, I pledged to her:
I can do nothing unless she concur.
Emilia, you must tell me what to do –
None can dissolve our sacred pact but you!
His fate hangs on your will, on your demands –
His life or death you're holding in my hands!
O gods, who made Emilia adored –
Make her, like you, content to reach accord:
Since I am powerless to escape her sway,
Dispose her to accept my wishes, pray!

(ACT III; PP 110–111)

Cinna

Pierre Corneille 1640
translated by Noel Clark 1992

Augustus, the new Emperor of Rome, has taken a violent and
bloody path to power. He has called upon Cinna to be his right-
hand man and confidant, seeking his advice on how, or if, he should
continue to rule. Augustus discovers that Cinna has been conspiring
to assassinate him, on behalf of his love Emilia, whose father
Augustus murdered *en route* to being Emperor of Rome.

AUGUSTUS

Heaven, to whom dare I, so sorely tried,
My inmost thoughts – indeed, my life – confide?
This power conferred on me – please take it back,
If having subjects means all friends I lack –
If that's the destiny of sovereign lords
Whose greatest bounty only hate rewards –
If your severe decrees crowned heads condemn
To love those you inspire to murder them –
Then nothing's sure and power supreme is vain!
Trust no-one, Caesar – and no more complain!
But why should I be spared, who all uncaring,
Soaked my hands in streams of blood, none sparing?
What oceans drenched the Macedonian field?
How much more blood at Actium was spilled?
More still, defeating Sextus! Then – a flood:
Perugia and its people drowned in blood!
Recall to mind, that carnage past description –
And add the blood-stained image of proscription,
When you dispatched those near and dear to you –
Seized your own tutor and then ran him through!
What right have you to brand the fates unjust,
If those who plot your death are those you trust?
In toppling you, by your example guided,

They're violating laws which you derided!
Their treason's justified, by heaven sired...
Forgo your grandeur, violently acquired,
Forfeit your faithless blood to faithless brood:
Nor thanks expect for your ingratitude!
But shock's unhinged me, left my brain confused –
Is Cinna pardoned and myself accused?
You, whose treason's forced me to retain
The sovereign power for which I'm to be slain,
You brand me felon, yet my crime condone –
Supporting, only to destroy, a lawless throne,
Your coup disguising with audacious zeal.
To tumble me, you'd scorn the nation's weal?
Yet even that, my bounty could forgive:
You've frightened me, but still I'd let you live!
No, no! Such charity outrages sense:
Who pardons easily, invites offence!
Assassins must die, accomplices be punished...
More blood be shed ... more tortures for the banished!
I'm tired of brutality, but can't prevent it;
Feared I would be – not all the more resented!
Rome's bred a Hydra, set on my disgrace:
One head I lop, a thousand take its place.
The blood of a thousand plotters I might shed –
Yet be no safer – more accurst instead!
Why wait till some new Brutus ends the story?
Better die now – and rob him of his glory!
Die! For life's a craven waste of breath,
If so many valiant souls desire my death:
Rome's noblest youth, of every generation,
Devotes itself to my assassination!
Their hatred I can't hope to cure ... so I
Must either slaughter everyone – or die!
What's life? So little of it's left to me,
It's not worth paying such a lethal fee!
So let me die – but dramatise my doom:
Let traitor's blood my torch of life consume –
Let him be sacrificed as I expire,

His treason punished, flattered his desire –
Yet tortured by the sight of my demise,
Knowing that he's been cheated of his prize!
But no! I'd sooner revel in his fate –
And if Rome hates me, triumph over hate!
O Romans! Vengeance! Power absolute!
O struggle waged by soul irresolute
That shrinks from every course it contemplates!
O gods! Your guidance this unhappy prince awaits:
Which path to follow and from which abstain!
Bid me destroy myself – or bid me reign!

(ACT IV, SCENE I; PP 119-121)

Bérénice

JEAN RACINE 1670
translated & adapted by Neil Bartlett 1990

Titus' father, the Emperor of Rome, has died eight days previously
and thus Titus is to become the new Emperor. Since he also wishes
to marry Bérénice, Queen of Palestine, his feelings are torn between
his desire and his duty: 'A Caesar with a Queen's something Rome
cannot conceive'. Titus procrastinates, for which Bérénice chastises
him, arguing that his own rights are as important as those of the
State. If he chooses Rome over her, she threatens 'vengeance' in her
own death. Titus is under intense pressure:

'Ah! Rome! Ah! Bérénice! Ah! Sad Prince! God above,
Why am I a Caesar! And why am I in love?'

TITUS

Madame, telling the truth is inevitable:
When I knew the moment was unavoidable
In which, ground down by the laws of austere duty
I should have to renounce the sight of your beauty,
When I first imagined the bitter goodbye,
My fears, your reproaches, that I'd fight, that you'd cry,
I then prepared myself to expect grief and pain
Such as I'd never felt or would have to again.
But whatever I thought, I don't mind admitting,
I didn't imagine one half of this feeling;
I thought I'd virtues enough t'uphold my name,
And when I think of how low I've brought it, I feel shame.
I've seen spread before me the whole of Rome assembled.
Senate addresses me; but my heart, enfeebled,
Listens without hearing, and gives them no response
To their effusive words but a glacyul silence.
Rome is still uncertain if you're going or not.
And I myself sometimes feel that I have forgot
If I'm still Emperor, if I'm a Roman too.

I came to find you here not knowing what I'd do;
My love forced me to come, and perhaps I came here
Just to look for myself and to make my fate clear.
What do I find? I find death here, stamped on your face;
I see you, seeking it, running to leave this place.
It's too much. My sorrow, confronted with this sight,
Has reached the lowest depths that it can reach tonight.
I am in as much pain as it's human to be.
But I can see a door ope'ning to release me.
Do not expect that I, defeated by my fears,
Will now propose marriage and neatly dry your tears.
For no matter how low you've finally brought me
My relentless Honour continues to haunt me;
The abyss which is fixed 'tween Marriage and Empire,
Tells me that after the public steps I've taken,
Now more than ever marriage would be mistaken.
Yes, Madame, and that I no longer have to make
Promises that I'll renounce the purple for your sake,
To follow you and run, happy to be your slave,
To the edge of the earth and to an unmarked grave.
If you saw me like that then you would blush too:
You would be embarrassed that in your retinue
Was a Caesar sans court, Emperor sans Empire,
A living monument, a Folly of Desire.
To escape from the torments to which my heart is prey
There is, as you well know, a braver, nobler way;
I'm instructed, Madame, down which path I must go
By more than one Roman and more than one hero.
When one grief too many wore down their resistance
They all interpreted the malign persistence
With which Fortune was bent on grinding down their
    might
As a divine order to give up the good fight.
If I must see you cry ev'ry time I draw breath,
If you remain resolved to seek out your own death,
If I must spend my days fearing you will end yours,
If you won't swear to let your life run its full course,
Madame, then other tears are soon in store for you:

In this state of mind there is nothing I won't do,
And I cannot promise that our bitter goodbyes
Will not be made bloody before your very eyes.
        No, nothing of which I'm not capable.
Now my life's in your hands and you're responsible.

(ACT V, SCENE VI; PP 57-58)

Le Misanthrope

MOLIÈRE 1666
translated & adapted by Neil Bartlett 1988

Oronte is rivals with Alceste (Le Misanthrope) for Celimene's love –
she's having a party full of ghastly, bitchy people. It's late in the
evening and Oronte's been left on his own. Like everyone else, he's
a would-be poet. His latest epic is a declaration of love to Celimene:
'My Love is like a Northern line station.
I get stuck on it'.

Oronte*'s solo; he interviews himself as if he was an author being*
congratulated on the publication of his new book by, for instance, Jonathan
Ross. *He plays both interviewer and interviewee, full parody of voice and*
mannerisms. This is, after all, the kind of thing people do at two in the
morning at parties.

ORONTE

Good ev'ning. I would just like to say, if I might,
That our first guest is looking pretty smart tonight.
D'you mind me asking if you have any special
Reason for looking so confident, so very cheerful?

I am young, I am rich, and of course the parents
Left me all th'Estate, plus some of their talents –
You have to realise, 'cause of my family,
That very few doors have ever been closed to me.
Intelligence and critical facility
Are things which I've always thought came naturally;
I remember that at a very early age
I loved the theatre – we'd a box near the stage –
Even as a child one was there on the first night;
One's judgement was precocious but, then as now, right.
I have always dressed well, dress sense is a talent
Which one either just has or one simply hasn't.

Everyone *likes* me; I'm never at a loss
Socially. Women like me. And so does the boss.
With all that going for him, I'd say, wouldn't you,
A man's entitled to look as good as I do?

But if Life in General is such a doddle,
Why's this particular bird giving you trouble?

Let's get this straight, shall we? I'm not the kind of guy
Likes a girl to lead you on then walk on by.
I'm a rich, busy man; it's not my style at all
To sit at home and wait for a woman to call.
Men like me don't love on credit; I'm keen, but still
I think, these days, one splits the emotional bill.
Of course, she's worth it; a rare commodity;
But men, just like women, want value for money;
Love has a price, and I'm pricey; surely, today,
No woman wants a man to give herself away.
We should balance the books – we should share expenses
As they're incurred in the battle of the sexes.

You seem pretty self-assured about the whole deal.

I've no reason to doubt the affection I feel.

Wouldn't it be truer to say this 'affection'
Is simply a classic case of self-deception?

Isn't all love self-deception?

(The interviewer is not satisfied with this feeble answer. The guest
collapses slowly into drunken honesty. God it's so embarassing when
someone tells the truth on a chat show)

    It's true. *(with a wince)*
                  C'est vrai.

What then makes you as confident as you say?

I tell lies to myself.
>   *So it's all conjecture?*
Desperate vanity.
>   *So in fact, you're not sure?*
No, I made it all up.
>   *So in fact, it's not true*
>   *As you claim, that Celimene's about to accept you?*

I don't think she likes me.
>   *So how d'you feel? Tell me.*
I'm very unhappy.
>   *Let's cut all the crap, shall we?*
>   *Right. Is she now, or has she ever been, in Love?*

(And of course we never hear the answer to this question, which is what we'd all like to know, because at that point, enter Celimene*)*

(ACT III; PP 90–91)

The Sisterhood
(LES FEMMES SAVANTES)

MOLIERE 1672
translated & adapted by Ranjit Bolt 1987

Chrysale's wife, a feminist literati, has just sacked the maid for being 'an ignorant, illiterate halfwit'. Usually, Chrysale is
> *'affable, he likes a quiet life,*
> *Which tends to mean kowtowing to his wife';*

but he plucks up the courage to chastise his wife, releasing his pent up frustration with her – and her entourage of poseurs.

CHRYSALE

Yes, it's you I'm talking to.
So quick to criticise, you fail to see
The full extent of your own lunacy.
If I were you, I'd burn these books of yours
(Except that set of Molières, of course –
They're worth a fortune) and I don't much care
For those outrageous spectacles you wear.
You've got things all mixed-up – your *rôle* in life
Should not be that of professeuse, but wife:
Why waste your time with all this bogus stuff?
As if running a household weren't enough.
A woman's proper place is in the home –
And not knee-deep in some portentous tome.
Once upon a time, no female dreamed of knowing
About anything but cookery and sewing.
Those were the days! That was the Golden Age –
A woman never read or wrote a page –
Her only library was a sewing box –
Her special subjects? Crochet, nappies, frocks.
But that's not good enough for you – your calling
Is to be Proust, Déscartes and Pascal, all in
One. You're forever wallowing in knowledge –

This used to be a home – now it's a college:
The servants don't do what we pay them to:
They're usually in seminars with you:
"Don't ask the maid to sew that button on –
She's writing an essay on de Maupassant."
"The chauffeur's not available today –
He's comparing Baudelaire with Mallarmé!"

(Act II; pp 93–94)

The School for Wives
(L'ECOLE DES FEMMES)

MOLIERE 1662
translated & adapted by Neil Bartlett 1990

Horace is a confident young man. He's left the city for the sticks
where he's discovered a gorgeous girl. He woos her, despite the fact
she's been locked up by her jealous guardian. Unknown to Horace,
the guardian is his uncle Arnold, who has plans to marry his ward
himself. With dramatic irony, Horace confides in Arnold and tells
him of his sexploits.

HORACE

I don't know how he got inside information
About Agnes's and I's little assignation
But he'd planned some sort of reception committee;
The window flew open – they all went to hit me –
And the next thing I knew, before I had had a
Chance – bang, crash, fell right off the bloody ladder!
There was slight concussion and some minor bleeding,
But I thus avoided a *serious* beating!
The servants – I guess on the old boy's instruction –
Then told him that they'd accomplished my destruction;
And since it took a while before I quite came round
I s'pose when they looked down and saw me on the
        ground,
Lying quite motionless, they thought that they'd killed me,
And of course they were a bit freaked out, quite rightly –
I heard them rowing as I lay there in silence –
Accusing each other of excessive vi'lence –
And then, in the darkness, I heard them come creeping
To check out if I was dead or was just sleeping.
Well you can imagine, in the dark, their worst thoughts
Were confirmed. I lay still ... I make quite a good corpse.
They finally left me – still rowing – rather droll –

And just as I prepared to abandon my role
Of the lifeless body – Agnes – she was crying –
Came running out of the house to where I was lying.
You see she must have heard the servants discussing
If I was dead or not; must have been listening;
And while they rowed, she took the opportunity
To get out of the house; it was all so easy!!
And when she found out I was *in working order,*
So to speak, she just ... I can't describe it, bless her.

(Arnold *in near apoplexy at this point imagining them having sex
on his lawn*)

Well, to cut a long story short, my beloved
Obeyed the promptings of her heart; she decided
She must leave her guardyun, give up the house, his wealth;
And now she is with me. In sickness, and in health.

(Horace *turns to audience*)

Ladies and gentlemen, is this not evidence
Of her guardyun's folly: she, in all innocence
Is forced to flee like this – consider the *danger*
She'd be in if it wasn't me, but some stranger –
But my feelings for her are as pure as they're strong.
I'd rather die myself than ever do her wrong;
She appeals to my better nature; and my heart
Is devotedly hers, until Death Do Us Part.
I know that Father will be furious. He's bound
To disapprove; but, in time, I'm sure he'll come round.
She's so sweet, that I just ... can't help it. I'm sorry;
Nothing matters in life except being happy.

I wondered if I – secretly, one understands –
Could place my darling charge, for a while, in your hands.
If you'd be willing to let her stay at your place –
Look it would only be for a couple of days,
The thing is, we need time to throw them off the scent

And work out a plan for our proper elopement.
If a young girl like her's seen with a man like me
People will put two and two together you see;
And if she was with you, well, you have been so kind,
I feel I can trust you, tell you what's on my mind.
I feel sure you'll help me. An old friend's advice is
Exactly what one needs in this sort of crisis.

(ACT V; PP 169-171)

Tartuffe
(LE TARTUFFE)

MOLIERE 1664
translated & adapted by Ranjit Bolt 1991

Orgon is trusting, generous, but gullible. He has been taken in by
Tartuffe's hypocritical piety, welcoming him to his household.
Everyone can see through Tartuffe and recognises his ulterior
motives (to steal Orgon's wealth and wife) – except Orgon. In his
eyes, Tartuffe can do no wrong.

ORGON

If you knew the man, I promise you,
You'd be completely captivated too:
Tartuffe's a man ... a man ... what can I say?
A MAN. You see, he's showing us the way
To inner peace – his mission's to expose
The world of Sense, with all its idle shows.
He's gradually opening my eyes
To the futility of earthly ties:
Wife, mother, children – I no longer care –
They could die now, I wouldn't turn a hair.

I haven't told you yet
(It's a heart-warming story) how we met...
He started taking the adjacent pew
To mine in church where, kneeling, in full view
Of a rapt congregation, he'd declare
His sins and launch into a passionate prayer.
Did I say kneeling? He was sometimes prone –
He'd humbly kiss the ground, and sigh, and moan,
And when I rose to leave, he'd run before
To offer me a blessing at the door.
His faithful acolyte enlightened me
About him, and his abject poverty;

I sent him ... contributions – he'd protest:
"It's too much! Take back half. I'll keep the rest
If you insist but, really, such largesse
Only exposes my unworthiness."
I'd make him keep the whole sum, whereupon,
With my own eyes, I'd watch him pass it on
To those more wretched than himself – until,
At length, he came to us. It was God's will
That this ... this paragon should share our roof –
That our affairs have prospered since is proof
Of that. Such is his deep concern for me,
No fault escapes his piercing scrutiny –
Especially my wife's – lascivious beaux
May flirt with her, but I'll be sure to know –
Where she's concerned, the jealousy he's shown
Over the past six months exceeds my own!
To his keen eye, the merest bagatelle
Is one more step along the road to Hell;
Things mortify Tartuffe that you and I
Would scarcely even be distracted by:
Last week he accidentally squashed a fly
(While praying) and you should have seen his guilt
Over the drop of insect blood he'd spilt!

(Act I, Scene v; pp 15-16)

Tartuffe
(LE TARTUFFE)

MOLIERE 1664
translated & adapted by Ranjit Bolt 1991

Having conned and wheedled his way into Orgon's household,
putting on an incredible, pious act, the hypocrite **Tartuffe** is now
trying it on with Orgon's wife. He slyly twists religious arguments to
woo her.

TARTUFFE
Though Heaven must have first claim on our thoughts,
The world contains attractions of all sorts:
They come from God, and everywhere our sense
Encounters marks of His beneficence.
The charms of womankind are Heaven-sent –
In you, those charms attain their fullest bent:
That face of yours was carved without a slip –
The summit of celestial craftsmanship –
A piece on which God lavished all His skill –
Call it His magnum opus, if you will.
Your beauty's manifold perfections vie
To captivate the heart and strike the eye,
As if their Maker wanted to rehearse
The timeless arts that framed the universe.
Yes! When I gaze on you, I seem to see
God's own self-portrait looking back at me!
At first, I was afraid that Satan meant
To tempt me – and you were his instrument:
Fearing for my immortal soul, I tried
To steel my heart, and to avoid your sight.
Then I reflected: *must* it be a crime –
Succumbing to a beauty so sublime?
Concluding that my passion could admit
Of chastity, at last I welcomed it.

I know it is presumption on my part
To offer you this paltry gift – my heart;
In doing so, I trust the merits *I*
So clearly lack, your bounty will supply:
There lie my fragile hopes, my peace of mind –
For life is torment if you prove unkind.
It rests with you – say, which is it to be:
Undreamed of happiness, or misery?

(ACT III, SCENE III; PP 39–40)

The Eighteenth Century

While Marivaux wrote challenging roles for leading *commedia dell'arte* performers at Paris' *Comédie-Italienne,* taking the performers beyond their skilled improvisation into dialogue of psychological complexity, Goldoni was reforming, reinventing *commedia* in Venice. His *riforma* threw off the masks and fleshed out the stock characters and pat plots, refined the coarseness of *commedia* and introduced motivated characters and plots.

Marivaux's plays might seem like frothy love intrigues, but his concern for narrative is with its subtextual subtlety. We play roles as a way of discovering emotional truth: the way we communicate, rather than the fact that we communicate, being paramount. Like Alfred de Musset a century later (a playwright greatly influenced by Marivaux), he picked up on the nuances and dynamic interplay of language from the *salons* which he frequented in fashionable Paris society. Where Goldoni's writing is bold and brassy, Marivaux's peels away layers of gossamer.

In Lessing's studies in theatre criticism, *The Hamburg Dramaturgy* (1767), he argues that the highly-charged emotions of *sturm und drang* can take place in a bourgeois drama just as much as in a play set in the past with kings and mythological figures as its protagonists. He had proved this on the stage over a decade earlier with *Miss Sara Sampson,* the first time German theatre had seen a prose tragedy taken from contemporary life.

Beaumarchais is satirical, charting the injustices of class and law and privilege through the tale of the benign but flawed Count Almaviva and his knowing manservant, Figaro. Within the social satire, Beaumarchais is rallying to progress. Casting his eyes incredulously across the 18th century, one of

Beaumarchais' buffooning characters asks (ironically): 'What has it produced that we should praise it for? Idiocies of every variety: freedom of thought, the laws of gravity, electricity, religious tolerationism, vaccination, quinine, the Encyclopedia, and plays...'

False Admissions
(LES FAUSSES CONFIDENCES)

MARIVAUX 1737
translated by Timberlake Wertenbaker 1983

Dubois and his master Dorante devise a scheme to marry
impoverished Dorante to the rich widow Araminte: Dorante is to
ingratiate himself as the steward in Araminte's household, while
Dubois becomes Araminte's servant and lays his master's love on so
thick that she couldn't possibly refuse him.

DUBOIS

You'll never believe the extent of his madness: it's
destroying him. He's of good family, with a pleasing figure,
fine features, excellent manners, but he's not rich. And yet,
there are countless women he could have married, who
were rich and lovely. They wanted nothing more than to
offer him their fortune, when they themselves deserved to
have fortunes laid at their feet. There's one in particular
who can't forget him and still pursues him. She's a very
vivacious brunette but he avoids her. It's useless, he turns
everything down. "I'd be deceiving them," he told me, "I
can't love any of them. My heart is elsewhere." And
sometimes there'd be a tear in his eye when he said this,
because he knows he's at fault.

Alas, he lost his mind one day as you were coming out of
the Opera. It was a Friday, yes a Friday. he told me he saw
you walking down the stairs – he followed you to your
carriage, and discovered your name. And when I found
him, he was still rooted to the spot, spellbound, in ecstacy. I
shouted at him. No answer. No one up here. Finally, he
came to, but he was still distracted. I threw him into a coach
and took him home. I hoped his folly would pass, because I

was very fond of him. He was an excellent master. But no, his case was desperate. That exquisite intelligence, that cheerful disposition, that sweetness of temper, you'd driven them all away. And from then on, he spent all day long dreaming of you and I spent all day long spying on you. I even befriended one of your servants. He was a most precise boy and could tell me everything for a bottle of wine. "We're going to the Comédie Française," he'd say. And I'd run home and make my report so we could arrive there an hour early. Or: "She's visiting this house, that house." And on that information, we'd station a carriage in the street for the evening so that he could watch you go in, and come out. He was inside the coach and I was at the back, but we were both shivering with cold because it was winter. He didn't even notice. I had to sustain my strength by letting out the odd oath.

In the end, I'd had enough. My health began to fail, as did his, so I told him you had gone into the country. He believed me and I had a little rest. But two days later, as he was walking in the Tuileries, mourning your departure, he saw you. When he came back he was so angry that – gentle as he is – he wanted to beat me. But as I didn't want him to, I had to leave him. I then had the good fortune to find a place here, but now he's found his way to this house, as your steward no less. Which, I daresay, he prefers to being Emperor.

You'd do him a kindness to send him away. The more he sees you, the more he'll deteriorate.

(Act I, Scene xiv; pp 26-27)

Successful Strategies
(L'HEUREUX STRATAGEME)

MARIVAUX 1733
translated by Timberlake Wertenbaker 1983

Frontin, the valet of Le Chevalier, undertakes his duties with relish, especially being used as a spy in a complex love mix-up. Dorante and La Marquise ask him to report on the assignations of their former lovers – Frontin's master Le Chevalier, and La Comtesse. He relays everything in great detail, much to Dorante and La Marquise's dismay.

FRONTIN

Let me bring forward the most trustworthy witnesses: my eyes, my ears ... Yesterday, the Comtesse and my master were taking a walk in the garden. I follow them. They go into the woods, I go into the woods. They take a path, I slip into the thicket. They talk, but I only hear unintelligible voices. I slide, I slither, and from shrub to shrub I eventually find myself in a position to hear and even see them through the leaves ... Ah! What a beautiful sight, cried the Chevalier. What a beautiful sight! He held in one hand a miniature and in the other the Comtesse's hand. What a beautiful sight! He's a Southerner, you understand, and I'm telling you this as a Southerner would, even though I'm from the North – one can do anything when one is precise and diligent.

Now, this portrait, of which I could make out the chin and a small part of the ear, was of the Comtesse. Yes, she was saying, they say it is a good likeness. As good as it can be, said my master, as good as it can be, but without those thousand charms of yours that I so adore, charms which a painter might observe, but cannot hope to reproduce. No, they belong exclusively to nature's paintbrush. Come,

come, you're flattering me, cried the Comtesse, her eyes sparkling with vanity, you're flattering me. No, Comtesse, let me choke if I do. I debase you by even daring to talk of your charms. Words cannot begin to touch upon them; no, your likeness is to be found only in my heart. Are there not two of us there, the Marquise and myself, answered the Comtesse. The Marquise! And where would she find room? You would fill a thousand hearts, if I had them. My love no longer knows where to put itself, it's overflowing, it must cascade into my words, my feelings, my thoughts. It spreads everywhere, my soul is bursting its banks. And so speaking, he sometimes kissed the hand of the Comtesse, and sometimes the portrait. And if she withdrew her hand, he threw himself on to the portrait, and when she asked for the portrait, he took back the hand. So the movement, as you see, went like this and like that.

To continue: Give me back my portrait, Chevalier, give it back ... But, Comtesse ... But, Chevalier ... But, Comtesse, if I'm to give back the copy, I must have the original as compensation. Oh, no, not that ... Oh yes, just that ... The Chevalier falls to his knees: Comtesse, in the name of your innumerable graces, give me the copy as security, while I wait for the person. Accord this refreshment to my ardour ... But Chevalier, to give away one's portrait is to give away one's heart ... I could endure having them both ... But ... There is no but, my life is yours, the portrait is mine, let each keep what belongs to him ... Well, you're the one who's keeping the portrait, I'm not the one who's giving it to you ... A deal: I'll accept the responsibility. It's I who have taken it, and you have done no more than allow me to take it ...

It was a sight to behold.

(ACT I, SCENE XII; PP 92-94)

The Venetian Twins
(I DUE GEMELLI VENEZIANI)

CARLO GOLDONI 1748
translated by Ranjit Bolt 1993

Pancrazio is madly in love with Rosaura; but she is to marry a rich
merchant's son, Signor Zanetto Bisognosi. Undeterred, Pancrazio
ingratiates himself with Rosaura's father while seizing the
opportunity to persuade Zanetto that marriage and women are the
worst things a man can endure.

PANCRAZIO

You are on the edge of a precipice. You did say you wanted
to get married? Unhappy man, you are ruined.

My only desire is to help my fellow man. I feel it my duty,
in brotherly love, to warn you: the step you are about to
take is an exceedingly rash one.

Marriage is a chain that holds a husband like a slave to a
galley. Marriage is a burden that makes you sweat by day
and keeps you awake at night. It is a burden on the mind
and on the body. And worst of all, it empties the purse.

And the woman who seems so beautiful at first – so gentle –
what do you think she really is? A siren who will lure you to
your destruction. Who will flatter you to deceive and plunge
you into penury. Alas, those flashing eyes of hers are two
furnaces that will reduce you to cinders. Her mouth is a pot of
poison, that slowly insinuates itself into your ears, seeps down
into your heart and kills you. Her cheeks – so soft and rosy –
there is witchcraft in them. Be warned – when a woman
crosses your path, she is a devil come to drag you down to hell.

Think it over carefully.

(ACT I, SCENE XVIII; PP 32–33)

Sara
(MISS SARA SAMPSON)

GOTTHOLD LESSING 1755
translated by Ernest Bell

Mellefont has led a rakish life, enjoying many relationships with
women. His latest passion is Sara, with whom he has eloped. They
have been staying at an inn for the past nine weeks. Sara is in love
with him, but is distraught that he will not make an honest woman
of her by marrying her immediately. Mellefont considers what is
holding him back.

After walking up and down several times in thought.

MELLEFONT

What a riddle I am to myself! What shall I think myself? A
fool? Or a knave? Heart, what a villain thou art! I love the
angel, however much of a devil I may be. I love her! Yes,
certainly! Certainly I love her. I feel I would sacrifice a
thousand lives for her, for her who sacrificed her virtue for
me; I would do so – this very moment without hesitation
would I do so. Yet – I am afraid to say it to myself – how
shall I explain it? And yet I fear the moment which will
make her mine for ever before the world. It cannot be
avoided now, for her father is reconciled. Nor shall I be able
to put it off for long. The delay has already drawn down
painful reproaches enough upon me. But painful as they
were, they were still more supportable to me than the
melancholy thought of being fettered for life. But am I not
so already? Certainly – and with pleasure! Certainly I am
already her prisoner. What is it I want, then? At present I
am a prisoner, who is allowed to go about on parole; that is
flattering! Why cannot the matter rest there? Why must I be
put in chains and thus lack even the pitiable shadow of
freedom? In chains? Quite so! Sara Sampson, my wife! The

half of the bliss is gone! And the other half – will go!
Monster that I am! And with such thoughts shall I write to
her father? Yet these are not my real thoughts, they are
fancies! Cursed fancies, which have become natural to me
through my dissolute life! I will free myself from them, or
live no more.

(ACT IV, SCENE II; PP 59-60)

Sara
(MISS SARA SAMPSON)

GOTTHOLD LESSING 1755
translated by Ernest Bell

Mellefont is a rake but has fallen in love with Sara, eloping with her to an inn, away from her beloved father Sir William Sampson. Mellefont's most passionate previous affair was with Marwood, by whom he had a child. Marwood is embittered by the direction of his new affections and plots to win him back by fair means or foul. Marwood informs Sara's father where his daughter is hiding and Sir William arrives at the inn. Marwood poisons Sara. Mellefont is distraught and wracked with guilt.

MELLEFONT

She dies! Ah, let me kiss this cold hand once more. *(throwing himself at Sara's feet)* No! I will not venture to touch her. The old saying that the body of the slain bleeds at the touch of the murderer, frightens me. And who is her murderer? Am I not he, more than Marwood? *(rises)* She is dead now, Sir; she does not hear us any more. Curse me now. Vent your grief in well-deserved curses. May none of them miss their mark, and may the most terrible be fulfilled twofold! Why do you remain silent? She is dead! She is certainly dead. Now, again, I am nothing but Mellefont! I am no more the lover of a tender daughter, whom you would have reason to spare in him. What is that? I do not want your compassionate looks! This is your daughter! I am her seducer. Bethink yourself, Sir! In what way can I rouse your anger? This budding beauty, who was yours alone, became my prey! For my sake her innocent virtue was abandoned! For my sake she tore herself from the arms of a beloved father! For my sake she had to die! You make me impatient with your forbearance, Sir! Let me see that you are a father! This angel enjoined more than human nature is capable of!

You cannot be my father. Behold, Sir *(drawing the dagger from his bosom)*, this is the dagger which Marwood drew upon me today. To my misfortune, I disarmed her. Had I fallen a guilty victim of her jealousy, Sara would still be living. You would have your daughter still, and have her without Mellefont. It is not for me to undo what is done – but to punish myself for it is still in my power! *(he stabs himself and sinks down at Sara's side)*.

(dying) I feel it. I have not struck false. If now you will call me your son and press my hand as such, I shall die in peace. (Sir William *embraces him)* What strange feeling seizes me? Mercy – O Creator, mercy!

(ACT V, SCENE X; PP 91-93)

Minna von Barnhelm

GOTTHOLD LESSING 1767
translated by Anthony Meech 1979

Just is the loyal servant of Major von Tellheim. The Major, a discharged army officer, has run out of money and can't pay the bills at the inn where they're staying. The major tells Just that they will have to part company. But Just fawns like a spaniel to his master, pleading to remain in his service. (He has a poodle of his own. And he tells shaggy-dog stories.)

JUST

Do what you like, Major, I'm going to stay with you. I've got to stay with you ... Paint me as black as you like; I won't think any the worse of me than I do of my dog.

Last winter I was walking along the canal at dusk when I heard something whimpering. I climbed down and reached out to the noise, thinking I was going to rescue a child, but, instead, I pulled a poodle out of the water. 'Fine', I thought. But the poodle followed me. Well, now, I'm no lover of poodles. I chased him off; no good. I whipped him away; no good. I wouldn't let him into my room at night, so he stayed outside on the doorstep. When he came too near me, I shoved him away with my foot; he howled, looked at me and wagged his tail. He's never had a crumb to eat from my hand, and I'm still the only person he'll obey, and the only one who can touch him. He runs in front of me and does tricks for me, without my asking him to. He's ugly for a poodle, but he's a wonderful dog. If he keeps on like this, I suppose, in the end, I shall have to stop hating poodles.

(ACT I, SCENE VIII; PP 107–108)

The Marriage of Figaro
(LE MARIAGE DE FIGARO)

BEAUMARCHAIS 1784
translated by Graham Anderson 1993

Figaro is the Count's loyal, though sceptical manservant. The Count
has been appointed Spain's Ambassador to London and is
encouraging Figaro to accompany him as his clerk: 'With sufficient
wit and strength of character, you could make your way up into
administration, eventually'.

FIGARO

Make my way by wit? No, be mediocre and crawling, and
you'll get everywhere you want. I know all about politics.

Yes, not that there's anything in it to boast about.
Pretending not to know when you do know, and to know
when in fact you don't; pretending to understand when you
don't understand, and not to hear when you do; and in
particular, pretending you can do things it's not in your
capacity to do. Then there's making a big secret out of
concealing the fact that there is no secret; hiding yourself
out of the way, twiddling your thumbs, and making out
you're profound when in fact you're an empty vessel;
putting on an act, good or bad; sending out spies and giving
hand-outs to traitors; tampering with seals and intercepting
letters; and trying to elevate shoddiness of your methods by
the loftiness of your goals – That's all politics is, and you can
hang me if I'm wrong!

(ACT III, SCENE V; PP 174-175)

The Marriage of Figaro
(LE MARIAGE DE FIGARO)

BEAUMARCHAIS 1784
translated by Graham Anderson 1993

Figaro is the long-serving valet to the Count Almaviva. But his loyalty doesn't stretch to allowing the Count *droigt de seigneur* with his fiancée, Suzanne, the Countess' maid. The Count has said to Figaro, 'dozens of times I've seen you heading towards your fortune, but never once in a straight line'. Figaro's had many jobs in his colourful career, including being a barber of Seville.

FIGARO

Did anyone ever tread a crazier path through life! Stolen by a band of brigands, I've no idea who my father is. I'm brought up to these bandit ways, but they disgust me and I want to pursue an honest career. And everywhere I go, I'm rejected! I study chemistry, pharmacy, surgery – and with all the weight of a great nobleman's recommendation to back me up, it's as much as I can do to get my hands on a miserable vet's lancet! – Weary of making sick beasts even sadder, I decide to go to the opposite extreme and plunge body and soul into the theatre. I wish I'd tied a stone round my neck and jumped off a bridge! I dash off one of those plays with a fashionable harem setting: you'd think I could poke a bit of fun at Mohammed without too many worries. Before I can blink an eye, an ambassador from heaven knows where complains that my piece is offensive to the government of Turkey, to Persia, to parts of the East Indies, to the whole of Egypt, to the kingdoms of Cyrenaica, Tripoli, Tunis, Algiers and Morocco. And there goes my play, up in smoke, just to please a few Muslim princes, not one of whom can read, or so I understand, and who spend all their energy beating us over the head and calling us "Christian dogs!" – Since a man's spirit can't be crushed,

they set about abusing it instead. — My cheeks started to
turn hollow; I owed a whole quarter's rent; I could see the
dreaded bailiff on the way, pen stuck in his wig. With a
shudder of fear, I try anything I can. A debate blows up on
the nature of richness, and since you don't actually need
first-hand experience of things in order to argue about
them, and since I didn't have a penny to my name, I write a
piece about the value of money and its net product. I
immediately find myself in the back of a prison waggon,
watching the drawbridge of a fortress being lowered to
allow me in, abandoning at its entrance all hope of freedom.

The carefree way they wreck people's lives! My God, I'd
like to get my hands on one of those jumped-up officials
when he'd had his pride cooled down by a disgrace of his
own. I'd tell him a thing or two ... The idiocies that appear
in print don't matter a jot until someone tries to block
them. Without the freedom to criticise there can be no such
thing as praise. Only little men are fearful of little
scribblings.

Then they grow tired of feeding an obscure gaol-bird and
throw me out on the street. And since a man has to eat even
if he's no longer in prison, I sharpen my pen again and ask
around to see what's new. And I'm told that since my little
holiday on the State, Madrid has set up a system of free
trade on all products, even extending to the press. Provided
my writings avoid all mention of authority, religion,
politics, morals, people in high places, influential
institutions, the Opera, any other public entertainment, or
anyone who has any interest in anything, I can freely print
whatever I wish, subject to the inspection of two or three
censors. To take advantage of this sweet liberty, I announce
the forthcoming appearance of a new periodical, and,
imagining I'm poaching on no-one's territory, I call it 'The
Daily Futile'. And, wow! A thousand miserable hacks rise in
chorus against me. My paper is suppressed and there I am
out of a job yet again! — Despair is about to overwhelm me.

I get mentioned for a position that comes up, but as bad
luck would have it, it suited me just right: they needed
someone good at figures, so a dancer got the job. The only
thing left was to turn to robbery, so I became a banker for a
card school. And, good people, listen! I dine out on the
town, and members of so-called polite society invite me to
their homes, retaining three quarters of the profit for
themselves. I could easily have reconstructed my life. I was
even beginning to appreciate that if you want to acquire
wealth, know-how is worth far more than knowledge. But
with everyone around me lining his pockets while insisting
that I remain honest, I inevitably landed up as before, down
and out. This time I was really going to leave the world,
and a dozen strokes out into the river would have settled it,
when a benevolent God called me back to my first and
original trade. I take up my strop of English leather and my
case of instruments. Then leaving the fog of dreams to the
idiots who thrive on it, and dumping shame at the side of
the road as being too burdensome for a mere pedestrian, I
barber my way from town to town, shaving and travelling,
and living at last without a care. A distinguished nobleman
arrives in Seville. He recognises me, I contrive his marriage,
and as he owes his wife entirely to my intervention, he
rewards me by trying to intervene with mine! And so
intrigues and storms. Ready to plunge into a terrible abyss,
on the verge of marrying my mother, my parents turn up
one after the other. *(growing heated)* There's a huge
argument: it's you, it's him, it's me, it's you; no, it isn't us.
Well, who is it, then?

Such a bizarre chain of events! How has all this happened to
me? Why these things, and not others? Who planted them
on my head? Forced to tread a path I've been set on
without knowing anything about it, just as I shall one day
have to step off it without any choice in the matter, I have
strewn it with as many flowers as my good spirits have
allowed. Yet I say good spirits, without knowing whether
they are really mine any more than the rest of me, or even

what is this ME I'm wrapped up in. A shapeless collection
of meaningless bits; then a mindless, puny being, a playful
little animal, a pleasure-seeking youth, with a taste for every
variety of enjoyment, undertaking every variety of trade to
earn a living. Here a master, there a servant, according to
the whim of fortune! Ambitious out of vanity, hard-
working out of necessity, but idle ... for the sheer delight of
it! A spinner of words if danger threatens, a poet by way of
diversion, a musician when the occasion demands, a lover in
fits of folly, I have seen everything, done everything, worn
out everything. Then the illusion shattered, leaving me too
disabused to ... Disabused! ... Suzanne, Suzanne, Suzanne!
How can you torture me like this! – I hear footsteps ...
someone's coming. Now we're at the moment of crisis.

(ACT V, SCENE III; PP 226-229)

The Nineteenth Century

Aleksander Fredro is hardly known in Europe at all, and yet he is 'the Father of Polish Comedy'. The comedy is a mischievous satire: of society, of social ills, of *nouveau riches* socialites. In the mid 19th century, Fredro's plays were welcomed as home-grown drama in a theatre dominated by the classical comedies of France (Molière) and Italy (Goldoni). Fredro's fun couplets owe something to these playwrights, and yet they look forward to the satirical plays of Russia (Ostrovsky). Such a distinctively Polish voice was also welcome in a country swamped by Russia, Prussia and Austria. Ironically, when his plays were premiéred they were censured for being unpatriotic; yet their patriotic resistance to occupying cultures have ensured their success in the 150 years since their first performance.

Unusually for 19th century plays, Fredro's comedies are in rhyming verse – this was the centruy of prose naturalism, which found its most comfortable home in the novel. Yet the Spanish playwright, Zorrilla, also plays with rhyme in *The Real Don Juan*. While we may be most familiar with the infamous rake Don Juan through Mozart's opera *Don Giovanni*, his legend is best known in Spanish popular culture through Zorrilla's play. It sentimentalises the character first born on stage in Tirso de Molina's Spanish Golden Age classic *The Last Days of Don Juan*. Zorrilla is just as moralising; where his differs is when Don Juan finally repents, recognising that there are greater forces than his own arrogant self:

> *'One moment will suffice*
> *To cleanse a lifetime's sin – and that is why*
> *For purgatory, and thence for Paradise,*
> *Don Juan is bound – GLORY BE TO GOD ON HIGH.'*

(Though this may, of course, be expedient tongue-in-cheek.)

Alfred de Musset was a poet as well as a playwright, and his plays are as lyrical as they they are graceful and witty. But these surface qualities – like the best work of the 18th century playwright Marivaux – reveal a deeper psychological insight when his characters bare their vexed souls. His plays were first performed as readings in the fashionable *salons* de Musset frequented: There he would have experienced subtextual anxiety lurking beneath surface propriety. They were only later performed on stage, when he regained the confidence to suffer public scrutiny after the failure of an early play. Yet his plays continued to raise hackles: *The Candlestick*, for instance, was removed from the *Comédie Française* repertoire when some felt awkward at its detailing of questionable moral codes. As much as de Musset's work is based on observation, it is also rooted in his personal life: from 1833-1835, he was involved in a tempestuous affair with George Sand (the *nom de plume* of the successful novelist Aurore Duoin – her private life was notorious; amongst her lovers was the pianist and composer Chopin). It is within this broad context that one can appreciate de Musset's curiously pleasing mix of potty scenarios, uncannily modern sensitivities, and subtle passion.

Nick Dear's wicked version of Ostrovsky's *A Family Affair* for Cheek by Jowl was not just a huge success because of a boisterous, leering production, but because it also scurrilously captured the spirit of late 1980's scamming, selfish decadence. Dear freely adapted the play: 'I have tried to make new jokes where the old ones weren't funny, and new plot where the old one chugged up a strange Muscovite siding of its own'. It was Ostrovsky's first full-length play and was immediately banned by order of Tsar Nicholas I because of its searing exposé of law and disorder amongst the merchant classes.

Zola was a novelist of the Naturalist school. The story of *Thérèse Raquin* was taken from a newspaper article, conceived as a novel, and then adapted for the stage by Zola himself. Pip

Broughton (the translator of his stage version) says that 'the play flourishes in the truthful portrayal of huge passions: lust, greed, terror'; and she adds: 'a huge intensity of playing and courage is required of the actors to make the text live'. The actor and writer William Gaminara's adaptation of Zola's novel *Germinal* is equally passionate on a personal level, but also embraces the resonances of political conviction in our own era. It is one of the first works of the 19th century which articulated the struggle between Capital and Labour.

The great Russian novelist Tolstoy wrote the play *The Power of Darkness* in 1886, but it was not performed until 1895, and then only with a revised Act IV. Tolstoy's quest to educate the Russian people in morality repulsed the Holy Synod. Tsar Alexander III, who initially thought it a wonderful play, later claimed (after the Holy Synod's complaints) that 'the play cannot be performed because it is too realistic and its subject matter too horrible'.

In the boulevard theatres of Paris, in the last years of the 19th century, Georges Feydeau was delighting the bourgeoisie with zestful, intricately-plotted exposés of selfish, sexual hypocrisies. The twist and turns and infuriations which fire the farce catch us between breathless anxiety – that our own infidelities are being revealed – and the wicked sneer of amoral glee. Feydeau's characters rattle through their dialogue, a frenzy which spills into the 20th century and onto its modern stage.

The Annuity
(DOZYWOCIE)

ALEKSANDER FREDRO 1835
translated by Noel Clark 1990

Leon's a hard-drinking card-sharp in a town of thieves, money-lenders and financial wheeler-dealers. He's down on his luck, but he's got life in perspective.

LEON

Lunatic? Not so! Should we
Not rather envy him, aloft,
As towards the heavens' canopy
Of stars, in his balloon, he'll waft?

What ecstasy – albeit brief –
Amid the clouds, sublimely swaying –
Man's many follies, so much grief,
With sage's thoughtful eye surveying!
And as he rises, higher – higher,
This globe of mud, our world entire,
This ant-heap we inhabit – all –
Will paltry seem to him – so small!
And we, proud ants, who would walk tall –
Full of ambition, knowledge, pique –
Just comic creatures – puny, weak –
Who, with a spark of life begot,
Upon our planet's level face,
Struggle to rise above the mean,
As though the earth they walk had been
By bolts of lightning seared red-hot...
Each clambers on his neighbour's back,
Heedless who's trampled in the race –
Whose heart, or life's condemned to plummet –
That he may rise, enhance his stature,

And stand, one day, upon the summit!...
(ironically)
Of this world's mighty deeds, what trace?
That once were hailed supreme to nature?
The blood and tears of mass attack –
The cheers of murderers victorious?
What price here, what there seemed glorious?
Where are the voices then upraised
That heaven might be duly praised!
High in the clouds, no sound – all's still;
The bliss of peace where none has trod!
Where one may breathe fresh air at will:
The further Man, the nearer God!

(ACT II; PP 298-299)

The Annuity
(DOZYWOCIE)

ALEKSANDER FREDRO 1835
translated by Noel Clark 1990

Watka is a notorious money-lender, pawn-broker, extortionist and miser. He is expecting to marry a young country girl of gentry stock. He's after some ready cash and is trying to sell a deviously come-by annuity (a grant) which is valid for as long as reckless Leon, in whose name the annuity is drawn, is living. 'I'm like a kitten on hot bricks,' says Watka anxiously.

WATKA

(with forced laugh) Never say die, John – stake my oath!;
Leon not well? That's nonsense pure!
Strong as Hercules! Mushroom growth!
Outlast Methusalah, for sure!
The way he's built! Why, what a frame!
His chest's enormous, head the same!
What bones! They're like a giant's, I swear;
You'll find none like them anywhere!
He's fighting fit, John, stake my oath!
Cross my heart and hope to die!

I'd like a word though, by the by
One little word ... and nothing more:
A hundred thousand, please – that's fair!

(Tvardosh shakes his head as a sign of refusal)

Ninety —

(Tvardosh shakes his head again)

Make it eighty then!

(Tvardosh *shakes his head*)

John, my dear fellow, valued friend!
You can't be serious! Heaven forfend!
Am I to be your sacrifice?
Don't squeeze me in a bloody vice!

Have pity, man! Some mercy show!
No conscience? No commiseration?
Sharp practice may work here below –
But spare a thought for your salvation!

Seventy, then!

(Tvardosh *refuses*)

If that's the way, sir,
Butchery is what you plot –
Better use a cut-throat razor...

(Watka *exposes his throat*)

Go on! Slice me – like a lamb!
Slay me quickly, on the spot!
I've lost my all! Destroyed, I am!
Or beat my brains out! Set me free
From sempiternal misery!

(Tvardosh *tries to leave*)

Make it sixty!

(Tvardosh *refuses again*)

I beseech,
John! May I lose the power of speech –

(Watka *points to his throat*)

My leg be shattered into four,
Bones be stretched until they break,
If I should bate a shilling more,
Or half a shilling less should take
Than – fifty thousand!...

(Tvardosh *attempts to leave;* Watka *responds hastily*)

    Forty, then!

What? Forty? Still the answer's "no?"
By the Maid of Seven Sorrows, deign
To pity me! You're merciless!

(Watka *almost weeping with emotion*)

I'm poor, the victim of distress;
All but ruined, brought so low;
Naked I'll stand – *sans* home or fitments –
To penury by you consigned!...
And I've got family commitments!
Aged father, mother blind;
Upon my breast, they'll breathe their last...
And soon I'll have a wife and children:
Pity, at least, my infant's plight!
Mercy on that blameless mite!

Johnny, for God's sake – life is sweet!
Don't put my family on the street!

(ACT II; PP 291-293)

Revenge
(ZEMSTA)

ALEKSANDER FREDRO 1834
translated by Noel Clark 1987

'Enter **Papkin**, dressed in French fashion. Sword, breeches, calf-length boots, toupet and kiss-curl, three-cornered hat, pistols in shoulder-holsters. Papkin always speaks very fast.' He has been asked by his friend the Squire to woo Clara on his behalf. But foolishly, Papkin believes he can win Clara's heart for himself. Papkin never doubts his own skill to impress:

> *'Papkin, Lion of the North and, since you ask,*
> *Distinguished officer, much decorated'.*

He embroiders everything he says – and, of course, Clara can see right through him.

PAPKIN

As in the far Arabian sand,
When Phoebus' golden rain descends,
And lily sears with scorching brand,
So that her pure white head she bends – –
When, garnered in the heavens blue,
To bring new life to withered brow,
Regenerating drops of dew
The famished flower with strength endow – –
So your sweet prescence here has been –
With equi-active, equi-potent charm –
A honey-flowing source of joy serene
(bows low)
To cheer your humble servant, ma'am!
For I, myself, might well have faded,
Had not your looks recovery aided.
Let now the gods controlling fate
Permit me to reciprocate:
And be – before Time's reaper calls –

Your flame – and then, the dew that falls!
(bowing low)

Oh, in the flower-bed of my heart,
Would that I might your seed induce
To germinate, put forth a shoot –
And there take ever-lasting root!

Surely, my costume and my sword
Proclaim me to be Mars's ward –
A man whose ever-chivalrous role
Has shuttled him from pole to pole!
Let Artemis, my trusty blade,
Whose steel the whole wide world dismays –
As 'twere a sponge – contused and gory –
Let it, in these more modern days,
Inspire your trust, proclaim my glory!

(with increasing ardour)
High on cliff-top's stony crown,
Where cannon weigh the ramparts down,
And bayonets raise a wall of iron –
With pikes and sabres for a vault –
There fights proud Papkin, like a lion:
God's champion, Devil's axe-man in assault!
Moan, groan, hack, slash! Around him – death!
Men crying "Mercy!" with their dying breath;
Maidens wring their hands in woe;
Mothers, children shriek with dread;
His sword-arm decimates the foe
And those alive are shortly dead!
(Clara snorts with laughter)
Forgive this blood-and-thunder tale
Of chivalry and virtues male!
No stranger I, to glory's portals!
I crave your leave to take my place
Among the ranks of happy mortals,
Whose talisman is lovely Clara's face.

Beloved monarch, Queen of beauty,
Ornament of all created:
Bid me "Jump into that fire!"
And, in the flames, your Papkin will expire!

(ACT II; PP 53-56)

Don't Fool With Love
(ON NE BADINE PAS AVEC L'AMOUR)

ALFRED DE MUSSET 1834
translated & adapted by Declan Donnellan 1993

Perdican returns home from university, eagerly anticipating
marriage to his childhood sweetheart, Camille. She, however, has
been educated in a convent and explains that she is intent on
becoming a Bride of Christ rather than his bride. He is saddened and
shocked: 'You are eighteen years old and you don't believe in love?'.

PERDICAN

There are two hundred women in your convent and most of
them have deep sores at the centres of their hearts. They
have made you stick your fingers in wounds, and your
virginal thoughts have been stained with their blood.
They've lived, haven't they? And they've shown you with
horror the course of their lives. You bless yourself in front of
their wounds, like before Christ on the cross. They make
room for you in their funereal processions and you squeeze
your body in between these desiccated cadavers with pious
hysteria every time you see a man walk by. Are you sure that
if the man who passed by happened to be the man who had
deceived them, the man who had made them cry and for
whom they suffer, the man whom they curse and pray to
God for at the same time, are you sure that the moment they
caught sight of him they wouldn't break their chains and run
back to their past unhappiness? Are you sure they wouldn't
press their bleeding breasts on the dagger that has slain them.
Oh my child. If only you knew the dreams of these women
who tell you not to dare to dream. If only you knew the
name that they murmur when their sobbing makes the Host
tremble before their lips. These aged women who sit so close
to you with their trembling heads, to spill into your ear their
withered old age. They who want to sound in the ruins of

your youth the alarm of their despair, and who crave the fresh smell of your crimson blood in their deep tombs. Do you know who these women are? Do you know who they are, these nuns, you wretched child? Who paint the love of men as a lie? Don't they realise there is something worse than that? That is the lie of divine love. Have they any idea that they are committing a mortal sin, to whisper into the ears of a virgin the words of a jaded woman? Oh what a good lesson they have taught you!

You wanted to leave without even taking my hand. You didn't want to see the wood, nor that poor little fountain that's staring at us in tears. You've denied the long afternoons of our childhood and the plaster mask that the nuns have strapped across your cheeks refused to give me a brotherly kiss. But your heart has won. Your heart has forgotten their lessons. Your heart can't read or write and it's brought you back to sit on the grass. Well here we are. Well, Camille, these women have done really well. They've really set you on the right track. It might cost me the happiness of my life. But tell them this from me. Heaven is not for them.

Goodbye, Camille. Back you go to your convent. And when they come out with their horror stories which have poisoned you, tell them this. All men are liars, inconstant, false, big mouthed, hypocrites, proud, cowardly, untrustworthy, animal. All women are treacherous, artificial, vain, prying and depraved. The world is no more than an endless sewer where deformed monsters slip and slide through mountains of shit. But in this world, there exists one thing that is holy and sublime, and that is the union of two of these horrible beings. We are often deceived in love, often wounded, and often wretched. But I go on loving, and on the very edge of the grave, when our past lives flash before our eyes, we can always say, "I have often suffered, I have deceived, but I have at least loved. I have lived. Me, the real me, and not some fantasy self, exhaled by pride and boredom."

(ACT II, SCENE V; PP 40–42)

The Candlestick
(LE CHANDELIER)

ALFRED DE MUSSET 1835
translated by Peter Meyer 1965

Fortunio, a clerk, has been used as a candlestick – the decoy in a
wife's affair to put her husband off the scent – by Jacqueline and her
lover Clavarouche. But Fortunio has believed Jacqueline's false
attentions to be genuine and, since he has secretly loved her for two
years, is deeply hurt to discover his role as a dupe.

FORTUNIO

In the ten minutes you've been speaking to me, you haven't
uttered a word that came from your heart. It was all about
your excuses, your sacrifices, your reparations! Your
Clavaroche and his crazy vanity! And my pride! You think
you've wounded my pride? You think that what hurts me is
to have been made a fool of and be teased at a dinner party?
That's not all I remember. When I told you I loved you, did
you think I had no feelings? When I told you of my two
years of suffering, did you think I was acting as you were?
You break my heart, you say you're sorry and that's how
you leave me. You've been forced, you say, to do wrong,
and you apologise. You blush, you turn away. You pity me
because I'm hurt. You can see me, you know what you've
done. This is how you cure the wound you've inflicted. It's
in my heart, Jacqueline, you've only to stretch out your
hand. I swear that if you'd wanted it, however shameful it
may be to say so, when you'll even laugh at it, I'd have
agreed to anything. God, I feel faint, I can't move.

I'm not witty or clever; I'd never be able to invent some
deep-laid plot when it was wanted. I was fool enough to
think you loved me. Yes, because you smiled at me and
your hand trembled in mine; because your eyes seemed to

seek mine and your lips opened and uttered a little sigh; yes,
I admit it, I created a dream; I thought that was how
women behaved when they loved you. What a fool!

I don't know if I'm awake or dreaming, and in spite of
everything whether you don't love me. Since last night, I've
thought over what my eyes have seen and my ears have
heard, and wondered if it were possible. Even now, you tell
me, I feel it, I'm suffering, I'm dying and I can't believe it
or understand it either. What have I done, Jacqueline? How
can you behave like this without loving me or hating me,
without knowing me or ever having met me? Everybody
loves you; you're good and kind and believe in God, you've
never ... Oh God, I'm accusing you, when I love you more
than life itself. Jacqueline, forgive me.

All I'm fit for now is to give up my life to your service and
whatever work you care to give me. I dare to complain, but
you chose me. I was going to have a place in your life. Your
lovely radiant face was beginning to shine on me. I was
going to live ... Must I lose you, Jacqueline? Have I done
something wrong, to make you chase me away? Then why
won't you go on pretending to love me?

(He falls unconscious.)

(ACT III, SCENE I; PP 110-112)

The Real Don Juan
(DON JUAN TENORIO)

JOSÉ ZORRILLA 1844
translated & adapted by Ranjit Bolt 1990

Don Luis Mejia and Don Juan Tenorio are infamous competing rakes. They have a rendezvous to decide a wager:
'Mejia bet Don Juan Tenorio
That in a given year (such was his whim)
He'd do more harm, more easily, than him'.
They meet at an inn to stake their claim to being the greater rogue.

DON LUIS

Like you, I hoped for inspiration
From an exotic field of operation,
And soon decided there could be no plans as
Fertile in opportunities as Flanders –
That breeding ground for territorial wars –
that hotbed of imbroglios and amours.
I hurried there. To start with, fortune frowned:
In less than one month, everything I owned
Was lost, and Flemings gave me a wide berth,
Seeing what I was (or rather wasn't) worth.
But, being of a friendly cast of mind
I looked about for company – I joined
A group of bandaleros – things went well –
We roamed the country, plundering pell-mell –
Then after numerous triumphs, off we went
To rob a bishop's palace down in Ghent.
That was a night, that was! His grace had gone
To the cathedral, for communion,
Leaving his coffers open to attack:
I shiver, even now, as I look back
On that stupendous haul! But human greed
Was all too quick to rear its ugly head:

Our captain tried to commandeer my share –
I challenged him, and beat him fair and square –
Three times I skewered him, like so much meat –
He fell, a bloody bundle, at my feet.
That showed the bandaleros what was what –
They voted me their captain, on the spot –
I vowed undying friendship, come what might. . .
Absconding with the loot the following night.

My quest for gold took me to Germany,
But there a Flemish friar spotted me
And gave my name to the authorities –
I was obliged to purchase my release.
I met that friar later, quite by chance –
Shot him – (of course) – and then set off for France.

On reaching Paris (what a city, eh!
The Naples of the North, as one might say)
I also advertised like this: "My name
Is Don Luis, and evil is my game:
Je suis prêt pour les femmes, et pour les hommes –
I handle both my weapons with aplomb!
Come one, *come* all!" And in my six months there
I proved myself a swine extraordinaire;
In every *cause célèbre* I played my part –
Raised treachery and mayhem to an art –
I won't go into detail, let's just say
I made my mark before I came away;
Ground reason, virtue, justice underfoot –
And broke a lot of female hearts, to boot.

I spent my fortune three times over, and
To build it up again, I've sought the hand
Of a certain Dona Ana de Pantoja,
A wealthy heiress form these parts – my offer
Has been accepted, and the wedding day
Fixed for tomorrow. (I hardly need say
You're very welcome.) All the things I've done
Are listed here – I'll vouch for every one.

(PART ONE, ACT I; PP 22-24)

The Real Don Juan
(DON JUAN TENORIO)

JOSÉ ZORRILLA 1844
translated & adapted by Ranjit Bolt 1990

Don Juan is a notorious rake, raping women and murdering for
wagers. After winning his last wager – to dishonour Dona Ines – he
had to flee Seville. After a Year in exile, he returns to discover his
father has died and
'bequeathed his whole estate
As a last resting place for those whose fate
Has been to fall foul of his butchering son'.
Wandering through the mausoleum, Don Juan sees the tomb and
statue of Dona Ines, the one girl he truly loved but abandoned.

DON JUAN
Clear air, unhindered room and solitude!
How often have I wasted nights like this
Deflowering some poor virgin I'd pursued,
Or murdering one of my enemies!
After so many years of decadence,
My jaded soul has been revivified;
This dispensation is divine – I sense
Not Satan, but an angel at my side!
(An unfamiliar familiar!)

Permit me now, you marble counterfeit
Of my beloved, lifeless though you are,
To lay my grief a moment at your feet.
Ines, your image comforted me through
A thousand dangers – now I curse my fate
For killing all the joy I ever knew,
And pour out tears of penitence, too late!
Ever since my departure, I have yearned
For one thing only – your divine embrace;

Heaven denied me, and I have returned
To find this cold, hard marble in your place!
Sweet girl, whose innocence and youth I blighted –
Witness my suffering through those eyes of stone –
Now, at the close, let our two troths be plighted –
Let Death, who parted us, now make us one!
You were the instrument God chose to bring
Goodness into my life – or is it your voice
I seem to hear, soothing my suffering?
Am I delirious? Should I rejoice?
And what I heard just then your parting sigh,
As heaven claimed my treasure for its own?
If God is up there, in that starry sky –
Describe my suffering – ask him to look down
On poor Don Juan!

(PART TWO, ACT I; P 74)

A Family Affair
(SVOI LYUDI – SOCHTSEMSYA!)

OSTROVSKY 1850
adapted by Nick Dear 1988

Lazar is the up-and-coming assistant to the merchant Samson
Bolshov. Bolshov's business is all bad debts, so he cunningly hands
over his assets to Lazar while trying to palm off the creditors with a
measly 25 kopecks for each rouble owed. The creditors don't bite
and Lazar reckons that he'll soon be out of a job. Seeking to save his
own skin, Lazar has an eye for a scam.

LAZAR

. . . It's a total disaster, it blinds me like a fog. I don't know
what the bleeding hell to do! The creditors called his bluff!
Twenty-five kopecks got laughed at! So now he's going to
have to declare himself formally bankrupt. Prison. Courts of
Commerce. Business goes to the wall. How will I survive?
Selling shit up a back-street? I've sweated blood for them
for twenty years, now they just let me go under? Like fuck!

Maybe I could sell his merchandise. Might find a buyer on
the Baltic. But wait. They say a man must listen to his
conscience. Well indubitably he must. However let's put it
in perspective. If you're dealing with a good bloke, of
course you pay attention to your conscience. On the other
hand, what if you're dealing with a swindler? Samson
Bolshov is one of the richest merchants in holy Russia. All
this is just a fiddle he's contrived for his own benefit. Me,
I'm a working man. Why should I care what happens to
someone who is, technically, a criminal?

I'm daydreaming again. Little Lipochka, or – what's her
formal name, no-one here ever uses it – Olimpiada – she's a
very highly educated young woman, you know. She's more

unique than most. But no posh suitor will take her without no bloody dowry! They'll have to settle her on a merchant. I've got prospects. Why shouldn't I go to Bolshov and say, "Sir, there comes a time in a young man's life when he starts to think about the furtherance of the line. Sir, your daughter – Miss Olimpiada – is a sophisticated lady, but as you can see, I am not exactly a yokel. Besides, I have some savings. I am respectful to my elders. Why don't you give her to me?"

If that doesn't work, I can always remind the old sod that I hold the deeds to his house and his shops ... It's amazing how that can move a man to a quick decision.

If I make a good case for myself ... A good, slick presentation ... I'll be walking up the aisle in a week. Fantastic! It's all starting to go my way! I feel like climbing up the bell-tower of Ivan the Great!

(ACT II; PP 36–38)

A Family Affair
(SVOI LYUDI – SOCHTSEMSYA!)

OSTROVSKY 1850
adapted by Nick Dear 1988

Tishka is an underpaid, overworked young servant of the nouveau
riche Moscow merchant Samson Bolshov.

Bolshov's *house.*

TISHKA

(with a large broom) Call this a life? Get up and sweep the
entire house before daybreak? Me? This family are
eccentric. I'm telling you. If any other boss employs a lad,
this lad lives with the rest of the lads – you're in the shop all
day, you get a little time to yourself. Here it's do this, do
that, come in, get out, I'm running through the town like a
lunatic. "Don't complain," they say, "you're lucky to be
learning a trade." Oh yeah. Very likely.

Respectable people keep a yardman for odd jobs. We've a
yardman here, too. Round about now he'll be lying by the
stove with the kittens. Or shafting the cook in the pantry.
So I'm the one who gets picked on. In respectable people's
homes the atmosphere's a bit more relaxed, like they're not
trying to prove nothing. Get in a spot of trouble, they say,
"It's all right, he's young." Here, you're held to account for
bleeding everything. If it's not the old man it's his Mrs. She
can't half dish it out. Or it's that creepy clerk Lazar. Or
dippy Fominishna. The place is full of low-lifes, pushing me
around. It's absolutely disgusting and intolerable. It's driving
me crackers!

(hits the furniture with his broom)

I'm going funny in the brains!

(ACT II; P 35)

Thérèse Raquin

EMILE ZOLA 1867
translated by Pip Broughton 1983

Laurent and Thérèse have murdered Camille – his colleague, her husband – to rid themselves of the obstacle to their frenzied passion. But they are tortured by their secret guilt: 'We have murdered our love,' cries Thérèse.

LAURENT

You're lying, admit that you're lying ... If I threw him into the river, it was because you pushed me into the murder.

Yes, you. Don't play the innocent, don't make me drag it from you by force ... I need you to confess to your crime, I need you to accept your share of the guilt. That gives me relief and calms me.

You were on the bank, and I said to you quietly, I am going to throw him into the river. You consented, you got into the boat ... You see very well that you killed him with me.

And, in the middle of the Seine, when I capsized the boat, didn't I warn you? You grabbed onto my neck. You left him to drown LIKE A DOG.

And, in the cab on the way back, didn't you put your hand into mine? Your hand fired my heart.

You intoxicated me with your caresses, here, in this room. You pushed me against your husband, you wanted to get rid of him. He didn't please you, he used to shiver with fever, you said. Three years ago was I like this? Was I a wretch then? I used to be an upright gentleman, I didn't do any harm to anyone ... I wouldn't have even crushed a fly.

Twice you turned me into a cruel brute ... I used to be prudent and peaceful. And look at me now, I tremble at the least shadow like an easily-frightened child. My nerves are just as wretched as yours. You have led me to adultery, to murder, without my even noticing. Now when I look back, I remain stupified by what I have done. In my dreams I see policemen, the court, the guillotine, pass before my eyes. *(he rises)* You play the innocent in vain – at night your teeth chatter with terror. You know very well that if the ghost were to come, he would strangle you first.

Listen, it is cowardly to refuse your share of the crime. You want to make my guilt the heavier, don't you? Since you push me to the edge, I prefer to make an end of it. You see, I am quite calm. *(he takes his hat)* I am going to tell the whole story to the Police Superintendant. We will *both* be arrested, we will soon see what the judge thinks of your innocence.

(ACT IV, SCENE VI; PP 82-83)

Germinal

EMILE ZOLA 1885
adapted by William Gaminara 1988

Monsieur Hennebeau's lavish evening meal is disturbed by a
delegation of striking miners from the pit which he owns. They
demand that he reconsiders the new rates of pay he has imposed
upon them. He is perturbed by the rumblings in the industry: 'A
new vision of society is being put forward ... We cannot sit back and
allow ourselves to be trampled underfoot.' He is a sly political
operator.

M. HENNEBEAU

Alright, alright ... let's look at this rationally. After all you
start by asking for one thing and finish up by asking for a
good deal more. A nine hour day? Not so long ago you
wanted a ten hour day and believing that to be an equitable
request we accepted; it seems we were in error for it would
appear that you have it in mind to work an hour less with
each year that passess. Is there no end to this? Furthermore
you say that you're going to lose per tub; now of course, it
may initially appear that way because you're not accustomed
to the system but believe me, in course of time, not only
will you make MORE money but you'll live longer as well.
(they all try to speak) ... I think ... I think we should be
honest about this, don't you ... conditions in the mines
aren't changing for the worse at all but some of the people
down there are; that's the real problem. Someone has been
promising you more butter than bread haven't they; well let
me tell you, if we had it we'd give it to you, but the plain
and simple truth is that we haven't ... and so these people
who are going around promising you this and promising
you that, they're the ones who should be blamed not us,
because that's the kind of conduct that threatens the very
fabric of our society, founded as it is and as it should be on

good-will and co-operation. So go ahead, have your strike fund, join if you so choose the great Workers' International next month when Monsieur Pluchart comes to see you ... yes, I know all about that as well ... but don't please turn to me when you find yourselves without employment.

(ACT II, SCENE I; PP 144-145)

Germinal

EMILE ZOLA 1885
adapted by William Gaminara 1988

Monsieur Gregoire is a wealthy man with a stake in the pits.
Returning from a day out with his daughter and friends he
encounters a march, protesting against pit conditions. A mob vents
its anger on the shopkeeper Maigrat who has extended credit to the
striking miners by accepting 'other means' of payment from the
miners' wives and daughters.

M. GREGOIRE

I was on my way over when they all arrived at once and
started to batter on Maigrat's door. They didn't notice me
... they were too busy pounding away with their fists,
bricks, anything they could lay their hands on, howling all
the while at the tops of their voices. Another couple of
minutes and the door would have given way, only just
before it did, Maigrat tried to escape across the roof; he
almost made it, only someone spotted him. They left the
door and straightaway started hurling stones and bottles, as if
he were a common cat. For a second I thought he was safe
but then I suppose he must have lost his grip, or else he was
hit by a bottle. Suddenly he started rolling downwards,
banging his head against the gutter as he went, and clawing
at the tiles to stop himself. He went straight over the edge,
landed on a wall and bounced back onto the road, right at
their feet. He must have died the instant he struck the
ground, but to look at them ... he might just as well have
walked out of his shop-door. I tell you, they fell upon him.
And kicked. And kicked again. I saw ... I saw them stuffing
earth into his mouth ... handful upon handful of earth into a
dead man's mouth! And then before I had time to think
what was happening there was a knife and they'd torn the
trousers from his body and were cutting ... cutting ... It was

only then that I saw Madame Levaque and I realised: they were all women. The men had gone on further into town.

(ACT II, SCENE VI; PP 178-179)

Germinal

EMILE ZOLA 1885
adapted by William Gaminara 1988

Souvarine is a Russian emigré, working as a miner in the pit where
Etienne is leading the strikes. When Etienne begins to lose faith in
the struggle, Souvarine inspires him with courage. Souvarine is an
experienced revolutionary: 'I should like to take the whole world in
these hands and crush it to little pieces, then we could begin all over
again'.

SOUVARINE

Did I ever tell you how my wife died? You see our plans
went wrong. We spent fourteen days hiding in a hole in the
ground, tearing the soil from beneath the railway line; but
we were given bad information, and instead of the Imperial
train it was an ordinary passenger train that blew up; eighty-
seven people were killed. Annushka used to bring us food in
the hole, she even lit the fuse because we did not think they
would suspect a woman. They arrested her six days later.
Every day after that, I followed the trial, hidden amongst
the crowd listening to every word that was spoken. Twice I
almost shouted out and leaped over their heads to join her.
But it would have been no use. One man less is one soldier
less and I could tell that each time her eyes met mine she
was saying no. On her last day, in the public place, I was
also there right at the back; she was the fifth in turn. Only
because it was raining the rope kept breaking over and over
again; they took twenty minutes to hang the first four. She
could not see me at first so I stood on a large stone and
stared at her until she caught sight of me. And from that
moment on our eyes never left each other, even after the
floor was removed from beneath her feet and her body was
left dangling in mid-air, her eyes continued to stare into
mine. And it wasn't until the wind turned her head to one

side that I was able to wave my hat and walk away. That was her punishment for lighting the fuse, and our punishment for loving each other too much. Now I know her death was a good thing, her blood will inspire heroes and heroines in years to come; and for me ... I have no weaknesses left in my heart, nothing at all ... no family, no wife, nothing that will make my hands shake on the day when they most need to be steady.

(ACT III, SCENE I; P 187)

The Power of Darkness

TOLSTOY 1886
translated & adapted by Anthony Clark 1984

Mitrich is a frail old soldier hired as a farm labourer by Anisya and
Nikita. Anisya has poisoned her first husband because she's in love
with Nikita; but Nikita has an affair with that first husband's
daughter, crushing their love-child to death when she is due to
marry.

Sleeping off a heavy bout of drinking, Mitrich awakes in the barn to
discover a suicidal Nikita despairing that the wedding is taking place.

MITRICH

Ah Nikita, you're a fool ... As foolish as a pig's belly-button.
(laughs) I love you, but you're a fool. You think I've been
drinking, don't you? Well, to hell with you! Don't think I
need you! Me, I'm a non – a non ... You couldn't say it
either! A non-commissioned officer in Her Majesty's very
first Regiment of Grenadiers. I've served my Tsar and
country with the greatest loyalty. But now, who am I? Who
am I really? You think I'm a soldier, don't you? A fighting
man? I'm not. I'm a soldier. I'm hardly what you'd call a
man. I'm an orphan, a stray. I vowed I wouldn't drink. And
now I've started to smoke!

Well, don't think I'm afraid of you, because I'm not!
Nobody scares me! When I drink, I drink! Now I'll drink
for two whole weeks, non-stop! I'll pawn everything except
my cross, I'll spend all the money on drink. I'll drink my
hat. I'll pawn my passport! And I'm not afraid of anyone!

The regiment used to flog me – to keep me off the drink.
They whipped me. Whipped me! "Well", they said, "are
you going to stop?" "No!" I said, I mean, why should they
put the fear of God in me? I am who I am. I am as God

made me. I vowed I wouldn't touch the stuff, and I didn't. But now, I've had a drink – I drink!

I'm not afraid of anyone. Because I don't tell lies like some people . . . Not even to myself.

Why should I be afraid of what people think? Scum of the earth, that lot! "Look," I says, "I AM".

A priest once said to me . . . . He said to me, "The Devil can boast better than anyone." You see, if you boast, it's because you're scared of what people really think of you. And if you're scared of what people really think, you're dough in the Devil's hands. He can do with you what he likes. Since I'm not afraid of people, it's easy for me – Easy for me to spit in the Devil's beard . . . And at his mother, the old sow-features. So there!

. . . Don't let people frighten you. They're the scum of the earth. You only have to look at them in the bath house to see that they're all moulded of the same dough. One has a fat tummy, the other's thin, that's the only difference. Why be frightened of them? To hell with everybody!

(ACT V, SCENE I; PP 86-87)

An Absolute Turkey
(LE DINDON)

GEORGES FEYDEAU 1896
adapted by Nicki Frei and Peter Hall 1993

Potagnac's been chasing Lucienne, his best friend's wife, all over
bourgeois Paris – from her drawing-room, via the farcical toings and
froings of the Hotel Ultimus, to a bachelor's boudoir. She's been
flirting with her husband's friend Redillon; her husband has
renewed his acquaintance with a Swiss old flame; and Potagnac has
been avoiding his own irate wife. On the morning after everyone's
night before, the *dénouement* is rapidly approaching.

POTAGNAC
Thank God! I've arrived in time.

What do I want? I want to stop you doing something
insane. I want to throw myself between you and Redillon.
Fight for you. Tear you away from him.

By what right? The right given but all the troubles that have
rained on my head since yesterday! My love for you has got
me into the most appalling mess! I'm up for two cases of
adultery which I didn't commit! Caught by a husband I
don't know with a woman I don't know. Caught by my
own wife with the same woman I don't know! My own
divorce pending. Another divorce between the woman I
don't know and the husband I don't know in which I'll be
cited as a co-respondent . . . A terrible row with Madame
Potagnac . . . The woman I don't know arrives this
morning to tell me in a Swiss accent that I owe her
reparation. A dispute with the husband I don't know
complicated by assault and battery. Turmoil, law suits,
scandal! Have I incurred all this, the whole lot,

everything. . . for you to throw yourself into the arms of another man? Is he to play cock of the walk while I'm left an absolute turkey! . . . Oh no, no, you couldn't want that! *(he breaks down).*

(ACT III, SCENE VIII; P 115)

Early Modern Plays

Austria: Schnitzler was writing in Vienna at the same time as Freud; he explores the amorality of sexual adventures through his egocentric characters.

Norway: Ibsen's characters reveal their inner selves when affected by external forces, such as a volatile political situation or when they flout social conventions.

Sweden: Strindberg's philosophical chamber plays, written at the end of his life, have pared down characters almost stripped of their souls.

Italy: Pirandello uses theatrical allegories for the disintegration of society and the individual in contemporary Europe.

German Europe: Ödön von Horváth is concerned with the nature of the individual in a continent dehumanised by war. Writing his sequel to Beaumarchais' late 18th century Figaro Plays, he is preoccupied by the paradox of freedom in exile.

These playwrights dislocate themselves from the certainties of the past and explore a vision of the future. Their characters dream of being giants or are scared of being dwarfed.

Anatol

ARTHUR SCHNITZLER 1891
translated by Michael Robinson 1987

Anatol enjoys the suffering of relationships with women of various classes. He is self-centred and arrogant in love. His confessor is his close friend Max, to whom he also retreats in moments of crisis: 'I can't live with my youth any longer. I'm leaving Vienna'. He has brought a parcel of mementos from his past conquests – 'letters, flowers, locks of hair' – to which Max responds: 'Nothing is sadder than yesterday's magic warmed up'. Anatol recalls one particular episode.

ANATOL

Well, I was sitting at my piano – it was in the little room where I lived at the time – in the evening – I'd known her for two hours – my lamp with the green and red shade was burning – I mention the lamp because it's part of the story.

Well! There I am at the piano, with her at my feet. That meant I couldn't reach the pedals. Her head was in my lap, and her tousled hair gleamed red and green from the lamp. I was extemporising on the piano, but only with my left hand. Her lips were pressed to my right –

There's really no more to tell. I'd known her for two hours, and I also knew that I should probably never see her again after the evening was over – she told me that – and I felt intensely loved at that particular moment. This love was like a carapace about me, the air was drenched and fragrant with it. Can you understand that? *(Max nods)* And suddenly this foolish, godlike thought came to me again – you poor, poor child! I was so clearly aware that the whole thing was – an episode. As I felt her warm breath on my skin, the incident was already a memory, complete, finished. It was in fact already over. She was another of the girls over whom I had to stride. Even the word occurred to me – that rather dry word – episode.

And at the same time I was myself – immortal. I also knew that the 'poor child' would never be able to forget this hour – it was clearer in her case than any of the others. It's commonplace to think – she'll have forgotten me tomorrow morning. But this was different: for the girl at my feet, I was a world; I felt a holy, everlasting love shining from her and quite enfolding me. This is something deeply felt, no-one can take it from me. I am certain that at that moment she could think of nothing else but me – just me. But for me she was already past, fleeting – an episode.

(EPISODE; PP 37–38)

The Wild Duck
(VILDANDEN)

HENRIK IBSEN 1884
translated by Peter Hall & Inga-Stina Ewbank 1990

Relling is a doctor who does what he can to help the poor. When the young Gregers devastates the Ekdals' house by exposing the lie upon which their happiness is based, Relling advises Gregers that his obsession with moral absolutes is inappropriate: 'The people in this house can't afford them'.

RELLING

I take care to preserve the life-lie. Don't you understand: a person's life-lie gives a point to his life. My method has been tried and tested. I've used it on Molvik as well. I told him he was "demonic". That's his particular therapy. What the hell does it mean, being demonic? It's just some nonsense, don't you see, that I've dreamed up to save his life. If I hadn't, the poor harmless swine would have gone under years ago in self-disgust and despair. And what about the old lieutenant? Though actually he's found his own cure. Well, what do you think of him, the great bear hunter – running round the loft hunting rabbits? There isn't a happier sportsman in the world when he can play with all that rubbish. There are four or five dried up Christmas trees that he has collected. And they mean as much to him as the whole vast living forest of Høydal. The cock and the hens are all the great wild birds that perch on the top of the pine trees. And the rabbits hopping across the floor of the loft – they are the bears that he tackles. He is the brave hunter of wide open spaces. If you take the life-lie away, from the average person, you take his happiness away as well.

(ACT V; PP 110–111)

Rosmersholm

HENRIK IBSEN 1886
translated by David Rudkin 1990

A new radicalism is exciting the young to rise up against the
conservatism of the older generation. **Kroll**, a biggoted schoolmaster,
is one of the latter. He has come to his brother-in-law Rosmer's
house – where Rosmer has withdrawn from his responsibilities as the
town's parson since the death of his wife – to tempt him back into
public service, offering him the editorship of the right-wing 'County
Newsletter'. Kroll couldn't edit the paper because 'Myself I'm told
stand even to be smeared a rabid fanatic'. Before asking Rosmer,
Kroll describes the political context.

KROLL

It's not possible to stand by a moment longer, look on and
do nothing. With this deplorable majority the Left have
won ... it's high time we ... And that's why I've prevailed
on our little circle of friends there in town to close ranks.
And high time too, I say!

No question but we should have acted earlier to stem this
torrent. But who could have foreseen what was coming?
Not I for one. Well, my eyes are well and truly opened
now. When the spirit of subversion has intruded into the
school, no less. Into my own school. Imagine! It has come
to my attention that my sixth-years – well, a number of
them – have formed a secret brotherhood and, for the past
term and more, been taking that paper of Mortensgârd's:
The Signalling Flame. I ask you, what diet is that, for the
public servants of tomorrow? But what saddens me most
about it is, they're all the best-talented boys of their year,
ganging together to conspire against me so. It's only the
clodpolls and backward ones who'll have nothing to do
with it.

Let me tell you: the undertow and subversion have
penetrated my very house. Into my own quiet home. And
utterly disrupted the peaceful family life I had. Think of it,
my own children...

In a word ... the chief conspirator at school's my son. And
my daughter has embroidered a red folder for hiding their
copies of *The Signalling Flame.*

No, who could have dreamed of it? In my own house,
where obedience and good order have ever been the way ...
where, ever till now, had prevailed the simple concord of
one common purpose...

(Act I; pp 84-85)

John Gabriel Borkman

HENRIK IBSEN 1896
translated by Peter Hall & Inga-Stina Ewbank 1975

Eight years ago, the disgraced **John Gabriel Borkman** – a visionary
banker who misappropriated clients' funds for ill-judged, empire-
building investments – was released from five years' imprisonment.
Since then, he has stalked the upstairs drawing-room of his house.
He had loved Ella, but she was sacrificed to his ambition and married
another (Borkman married Ella's sister). Despite an awareness of
reality – 'it is iron-hard and free from dreams' – he still believes in his
power 'to create human happiness, in ever-widening circles around
me'. He is a tragic hero; we see him long after his fall, in his last
moments, in the snow-covered grounds of his house.

BORKMAN

Listen, down there by the river, Ella ... the factories are
at work! My factories. All the factories I wanted to build.
Listen to them, working the night shift ... yes, they're
working night and day. Listen, listen! The wheels whirl, the
cylinders flash ... round and round and round! Can't you
hear them Ella? I can.

(more and more fired with enthusiasm) But all these are only the
foothills of the kingdom, you know. The kingdom I was
about to take possession of when I ... when I died. And
now it lies there ... without a ruler, defenceless. Open to the
attacks of thieves and plunderers. Ella ... do you see the
peaks of the mountains ... there ... far away? One behind
the other. Rising. Towering. They are my vast,
inexhaustible kingdom. My kingdom-without-end...

An icy wind comes from that kingdom. To me, that wind is
the breath of life. It is a greeting from the spirits that serve
me. I sense them ... earth-bound millions. I feel them ...

veins of iron-ore, stretching out their arms to me ...
branching, beckoning, enticing. I saw them before me,
phantoms flickering into life ... the night I stood in the
vaults of the bank, the lantern in my hand. *(pause)* You
longed to be freed then. I tried. But I lacked the power.
Your treasure sank back into the depths. *(hands reaching out)*
But I'll whisper to you here in the stillness of the night: I
love you, as you lie like the dead, deep in the darkness! I
love you, you riches longing for life ... your retinue a blaze
of power and of glory. I love you, I love you, I love you.

(ACT IV; PP 215-216)

The Black Glove
(SVARTE HANDSKEN)

AUGUST STRINDBERG 1907
translated by Eivor Martinus 1991

In the apartment block which dominates all of Strindberg's Chamber
Plays (as if it were a ship of life) the **Christmas Spirit** describes
how he oversees the lives of its inhabitants:

'I am the custodian of law and order in this house,
I punish, comfort, strike and love ... and clean up'.

CHRISTMAS SPIRIT

I have a big house to look after.
A Tower of Babel with all kinds of people
and languages; six flights of stairs and a basement;
three apartments on each floor,
a dozen cradles and seven pianos:
many people's destinies have been decided here;
hearts and minds and tempers pull and strain
like rocks and rafters.
It hangs together but just about...
and the neighbour – who doesn't know his next-door
            neighbour
must learn to tolerate and show forbearance...
overlook his neighbour's little whims.
One plays the piano after ten,
one rises too early, one's too late to bed.
It can't be helped, one has to compromise;
listen to all those little noises
in the stairwell shell...
The lift is creaking, the pipes are gurgling...
and the central heating simmers like a samovar;
Listen ... someone's using the shower,
there goes the vacuum cleaner.
A door is shut, a little child is crying,

here a newly-wed, there a divorcee,
and over there a widower.
Jumbles up like their pianinos
between them producing a waltz,
a fugue and a sonata.
In the basement ... poverty like in the attic,
in the apartments ... luxury and show,
solid assets and hollow lives.
People make a living, surge forward, scrape along,
one day someone dies, someone else gets married
and another sues for divorce.
Someone quarrels, moans, makes up...
but when he realises the struggle is to no avail
he takes his leave and moves away.

(SCENE I; P 198)

After the Fire
(BRÄNDA TOMTEN)

AUGUST STRINDBERG 1907
translated by Eivor Martinus 1991

After thirty years, the **Stranger** has returned from America to
discover that his family home, where his brother still lives, has just
burned down. (The student lodger who has been accused of arson is
the Stranger's secret, illegitimate son.) The Stranger rummages
through the wreckage, the rubble of his youth, while all the locals
stand by gawping.

STRANGER

There they stand gloating over the disaster, waiting for the
victim which seems to be the main thing. They regard it as
a fact that it must be a case of arson, because that is what
they wish it to be. And all these crooks are my friends from
my youth, companions ... I'm related to the hearse-driver
through my stepmother whose father carried corpses for a
living ... Don't stand there, my friends ... there could be
dynamite in the cellar and we might have an explosion any
minute. *(the crowd disperses)*

These books belong to the student. The same rubbish as in
my youth. Livy, Roman history ... which is supposed to be
a pack of lies, but here is a book from my brother's
collection. 'Columbus or the man who discovered
America.' That's my book ... which I got for Christmas in
1857, the name is rubbed out, someone stole it from me ...
and I accused one of the maids who was subsequently
dismissed. A fine thing, maybe that was her downfall. Fifty
years ago ... There is the frame for the family portrait; my
splendid grandfather, the smuggler ... who was in chains.
Fine thing! But what's this? The bedstead belonging to the
mahogany bed ... the bed where I was born! Damn. Item:

The legs of a dining table ... an heirloom ... yes, we were told it was of solid ebony, we admired it and now fifty years later it's proved to be of stained maple. Everything in our home was stained, to make it unrecognisable ... and our clothes were dyed when we were children, so we were always walking around with our bodies stained from the dye. Bluff ... ebony. Here is the big clock ... also contraband goods ... which measured out the time for two generations, was wound up every Saturday when we were given dried cod and a small beer for dinner ... like a clever clock it used to stop every time someone died. Let me have a look at you. Let's see how you look inside, old friend. Breaks at the touch. That's how it was with everything. Vain, futile. Here is the globe which used to be at the top, but it should have been underneath. You little earth, the densest of all the planets and the heaviest, making it so hard for you to breathe, hard to carry your burden; the cross is your symbol, but it could equally well have been a fool's cap or a strait-jacket ... the world of illusions and madmen.

Oh Eternal One, has your earth got lost in space? And how did it come to spin so fast that your children got giddy and lost their senses ... so they couldn't see the real thing but only that which appeared real. Amen.

(SCENE II; PP 85-86)

The Pelican
(PELIKANEN)

AUGUST STRINDBERG 1907
translated by Eivor Martinus 1991

Frederik drunkenly confronts his mother (the pelican of the title)
who has starved and tyrannised her son and daughter Gerda. Their
father has died, but has left a letter revealing the extent of their
mother's wickedness. Frederik argues that their mother has murdered
them all in spirit.

THE SON

Listen mother, if I was sober I wouldn't answer truthfully
because I wouldn't have the strength but now I'm going to
tell you that I have read father's letter which you stole and
threw on the fire...

I remember when you taught me to lie for the first time. I
could hardly speak, do you remember? And when you lied
to me for the first time. I also remember once when I was a
child ... I had hidden under the piano and then a lady came
to see you. You sat there, lying to her for three hours and I
had to listen to you.

But do you know why I am so wretched? I was never
breast-fed, you gave me a nanny and a bottle instead; and
when I got older nanny took me to her sister's and she was
a prostitute; and there I witnessed the most intimate scenes,
the kind that usually only dog owners show children in the
street in spring and autumn. When I told you about it ... I
was four at the time ... when I told you what I had seen in
that den of vice you said I was lying and you hit me as if I'd
been lying even though I spoke the truth. This maid –
encouraged by you – initiated me into all the secrets when I
was five years old ... I was only five ... *(he sobs)* And then I

starved and froze, like father and the rest of the family. And it's only now ... all these years later ... I learn that you stole from the housekeeping money and the money for the heating ... look at me, pelican, look at Gerda who hasn't got a chest. You know perfectly well how you murdered my father, you know ... because you brought him to despair which is not a crime punishable by law; you know yourself how you've murdered my sister, but now she realises it as well.

(sobs) It's terrible to have to say all this, but I had to. I know that when I'm sober again I'll shoot myself, that's why I carry on drinking. I don't dare get sober...

(SCENE IV; PP 179-180)

The Great Highway
(STORA LANDSVÄGEN)

AUGUST STRINDBERG 1909
translated by Eivor Martinus 1990

As The Hunter goes on a spiritual journey through the Alps,
accompanied some of the way by The Wanderer, he encounters all
sorts of oddballs. One is the **Schoolmaster** – so sane that he only
manages to fit in by appearing insane.

SCHOOLMASTER

Abra-cadabra, abracadabra, ab-ra-ca-dab-ra! No! They didn't
hear. Once again: Abra-ca-dabra, abra-cadabra, abra-ca-dabra. No, these toffee-nosed people know how to restrain
themselves. Gentlemen, he who doesn't venture an opinion
must be presumed to agree with me. Will you accept a
challenge from the most prominent intellectual individuals of
this village? They'd like to challenge you both to a verbal
duel. If I don't get a response I presume the answer to be in
the affirmative. One, two, three.

I'm the only sane person in this village. That's why I have to
play the fool – to avoid being locked up. I have an academic
education; I have written a tragedy in five acts, a verse drama.
It's called 'Potamogeton'. It's so damn stupid that I ought to
have won the first prize for it but the local blacksmith
surpassed me in stupidity and submitted a homage to the
Destroyer of the Country, so I didn't get a prize after all.

They ignore me, you see. You probably think I'm selfish
talking about myself, but I have two reasons for this. Firstly, I
have to introduce myself to you, secondly you wouldn't be
too pleased if I talked about you, would you now? Here is
the blacksmith. I'd better put on my disguise or he'll think
I'm perfectly normal and then he'll have me locked up.

Neither rhyme nor reason. Life is a battle and we're all soldiering on. Two times two make four and six more make eight. Do you get it?

(SCENE III; PP 27-28)

The Great Highway
(STORA LANDSVÄGEN)

AUGUST STRINDBERG 1909
translated by Eivor Martinus 1990

The Hunter wanders through the Alps on a spiritual journey to
'The Land of Fulfilled Wishes'. His encounters with symbolic
characters make him recall those he has met throughout his life. He
struggles with his soul; he resists temptations. He is a pilgrim
enduring his last hours in this world: 'I struggle, therefore I live. I
don't exist, only what I've done exists'.

HUNTER
I look distraught because I've had my head turned. I used to
take people at face value; that's why I've been filled with
lies. Everything that I used to believe in turned out to be
lies. That's why I too am a fraud. I've roamed about with
false opinions of people and life in general. I've worked
with false premises, and passed counterfeit coins without
knowing it. That's why I'm not the one I seem to be. I
can't be with other people, I can't speak, not even on
someone else's behalf, I can't appeal to a testimony without
worrying that it may be a lie. On several occasions, I've
been an accomplice in the anchor chain called society, but
when I started to resemble all the others, I decided to
become a man of the forest, a highwayman.

I don't have long to live and I want to be alone when I
settle my accounts...

Bring me despair,
you who want to tempt me into denying
the existence of our merciful Lord.
I came down here from pure mountain air in the Alps
to be among the people for a little longer

and share their problems but there was no open road,
just an aperture through thorny thickets...
I left a piece of clothing here and there
and got entangled in the shrubbery.
People gave in order to take back with interest...
They gave in order to turn gifts into debts...
People served you in order to command...
set you free in order to enslave you...
I lost my travelling companion along the way,
One trap followed upon the other
and I was sucked into mill-wheels,
came out the other end...
was shown a beacon in a child's eye...
which guided me to this place in the darkness.
And now you're handing me the bills.

I am alone!
In nocturnal darkness...
where the trees are fast asleep and the grass is weeping
with cold after the sun's gone down,
but the animals are keeping watch, not all, however.
The bat is plotting and the serpent wriggles
under poisonous mushrooms,
a badger, shunning the light, stirs
after a long day's sleep.
Alone! – Why? ...
A traveller in other people's countries
is always a stranger, alone.
He passes through towns and villages,
puts up at hotels, checks out and moves on
until the journey is over ... then he is home again!
But it's not over...
I can still hear ... a dry branch
snapping ... and an iron heel against the rock...
it's the formidable blacksmith
the idolator, with his flint knife...
he is looking for me...
and the miller with his mill-wheel

where I was sucked in
and almost got stuck...
The people of the shopping arcade
the people...
a net so easy to get caught in
but hard to escape from...
And the murderous Mr Möller
with his bills and law suits
and alibis and libels
the man without honour...
What's that noise? It's music! I recognise the notes...
I recognise the notes ... and your little hand
I have no desire to meet...
the fire is comfortably warm at a distance,
if you get too close, it will burn you.
And now: a child's voice in the dark!
You dear child, my last bright memory
that will follow me into the forest of the night,
on my final journey to the distant land,
The Land of Fulfilled Wishes,
which seemed like a mirage from the Alps
but vanished when I reached the valleys...
concealed by road dust ... chimney smoke.
Where did you disappear to ... lovely vision,
land of yearning and of dreams?

If only a vision I want to see you once again,
from the snowy peak in the crystal clear air...
at the hermit's place ... where I shall stay
and wait to be released...
I hope he'll make some space
under his cold white blanket:
and then he'll draw a fleeting epitaph in the snow:
'Here rests Ishmael, Hagar's son
once called Israel,
because he struggled with God
and didn't let go until overcome...
defeated by his omnipotent goodness'.

Oh eternal one! I won't let go of your hand,
your hard hand, unless you bless me!

Bless me, your poor mankind,
who suffers, suffers from your gift of life!
Me first who's suffered most
who's suffered most and grieved
because I couldn't be the man I'd hoped to be!

(SCENE VII; PP 61-64)

The Rules of the Game
(IL GIUOCO DELLE PARTI)

PIRANDELLO 1918
translated & adapted by David Hare 1992

At the request of his wife Silia, **Leone** has lived alone for three years
with his books and his cooking, allowing her some freedom. He
visits her for half an hour each evening, though he never goes up the
stairs. This evening, Silia is at home with her lover, Guido. When
her husband arrives, she asks him to come up, leaving Guido to face
him alone. Guido finds Leone unnerving: 'You insist on behaving as
if you don't exist. Which is extremely confusing and utterly
pointless'.

LEONE

You're right. Of course. I ought not to exist. In fact I
promise you that I do my utmost to exist as little as possible.
Not just for other peoples' benefit but for my own. But the
blame goes back a very long way. Back to the very fact I
was born. There we are. I'm imprisoned for life. I exist. It's
a fact. Other people should take that much into account
because there's nothing I can do. I'm on earth. At least for a
while. I married Silia. Or, rather, let's be accurate, I let her
marry me. Another fact: another prison. What can you do?
Almost at once she became unhappy, she started to
complain, to fret, to panic, to twist. Guido, I tell you, she
was desperate to escape. And I ... I promise you, you must
believe me ... I was deeply hurt. Then we hit on this
solution. I left her here with everything. I just took my
books and my saucepans. Life without saucepans, Guido:
unthinkable. But I know it's no good. I am stuck with my
role. I married her. It's a fact. My part is: the husband.
Perhaps people should take that into account also.
However.

(there is a pause)
You know how it is with the blind? The blind are never
next to anything. If you tell a blind man who's feeling
round for something, "you've got it there, just beside you,"
he'll immediately turn his whole body to face it. And that
woman is like that. She's never alongside you. She's always
opposite.

(ACT I, SCENE III; PP 15-16)

Man, Beast & Virtue
(L'Uomo, la Besta e la Virtu)

Luigi Pirandello 1919
new version by Charles Wood 1989

Paolina is a quack professor tutoring a 'monkey' and a 'goat' – two put-upon pupils – in his ramshackle house crammed with thousands of books. He is a bundle of harassed, nervous energy.

PAOLINO
What ... is the Greek for actor don't look at your vocabularies ... you? ... You don't know. You? ... Whoops, slipped your mind has it? You mean you did know once, but, whoops, slipped, doesn't come to mind now? ... Well, what you should say is: I – do – not – know! I – do – not – know! Not, whoops slipped my ... I will tell you what it is. The Greek for actor is upocritès. There. Why? Why upocritès? What do actors do? ... Not sure? ... Do you think it's fair to call an actor doing his job acting a hypocrite? Doing his job, pursuing his profession. You can't call him a hypocrite for that. Who can you call a hypocrite then, this word the Greeks gave their actors? You ... Somebody who pretends ... Right. Just like an actor pretends to be a king, an emperor even, when he hasn't got two coins to rub together in real life, when he is penniless, in a tinsel crown ... You jeer. What do you jeer at? An actor does his job, there's nothing wrong with an actor doing his job. When is it wrong? I'll tell you, when it's malicious, when it's habit, when one is not an actor but a person going about the business of life; when it is to one's smiling advantage to pretend. Out of politeness, because being polite is to pretend; and how we do it, our souls black as night, as the feathers of a crow inside but outside white as those of a dove; inside one's throat the bitterness of gall, on one's lips the sweetness of honey; and such as: "Good morning, sir"

instead of: "Go to hell, sir!", eh? ... Because being polite insists that we wish good morning to somebody we would willingly consign to hell. Being polite means being a hypocrite. *Quod erat demonstrandum!* Now, history.

(ACT I; PP 17-19)

The Mountain Giants
(I GIGANTI DELLA MONTAGNA)

LUIGI PIRANDELLO 1936
new version by Charles Wood 1993

Cotrone is a theatrical magician who has rejected the real world of
praise and esteem for his art. He lives with others like him in the
Villa Scalonga, as their benevolent leader. He is introducing his new
world to a group of travelling players.

COTRONE

Your world once held me and I could have been something
as they say, gone to the top, had I not retired, resigned, left
decorum, honour, dignity, virtue hanging on pegs ... once
you've jerked that lot off if you've still got a soul it does feel
very lively and large, like air with sunshine and clouds open
to lightning strikes, thunder bolts, winds light, slight or
monstrous, the superfluous stuff of marvels whirling into
mystery, fabulous longinquity. Look down there at sad Earth
where some think they live their own lives and don't come
near. The body you see is not what there is it's only the soul
can speak of what there is and, who knows from where the
soul gets its words? We're appearances through appearances
to appearances with funny names like Cotrone, like Doccia
... like Quaqueo ... a body is a corpse benighted, and stone.
I wouldn't like to be the man who thinks he's there in his
body with his name, would rather be the very first ghost
comes into my head, to moan. We've inherited some, like
the braw wee Scots lassie with the umbrella. How she got
here we'll never know but the punters expect it. And
there's an occasional guest appearance of the blue nosed
dwarf. Specialities of the house ... They come with the villa
but, everything else is ours. With the divine prerogative
given children to play and live their games excluding all else
we let that which is in us come out, and live it, sometimes

teetering on delicious insanity. So, let me tell you what was once told pilgrims; kick off your sandals you've arrived!

(ACT II; PP 53-54)

Figaro Gets Divorced
(FIGARO LÄSST SICH SCHEIDEN)

ÖDÖN VON HORVATH 1937
translated by Ian Huish 1990

Figaro is valet to the Count Almaviva; his wife, Susanne, maid to
the Countess. Together they have all fled across the border, away
from the revolution. Despite dwindling resources, the Almavivas
insist on living the life to which they are accustomed. After three
months they have to sell their pearls to pay the bills of an expensive
mountain health resort. Figaro complains to Susanne. He is a man
who has always lived on his wits.

FIGARO

How long can we afford this luxurious life-style our masters
are indulging in? Till Easter, and what then? Then there
won't be any more pearls to cast before the swine like we've
done up till now! *(leaping up)* I can't listen to any more of
this drivel! Three months ago he said it'd be over in two
months. Drivel! Eight weeks ago he said it'd all be over in
six weeks. Drivel. Four weeks ago he said we'd be home by
Christmas and Christmas is the day after tomorrow. Drivel
again. I tell you it's all a load of drivel, the situation's
stabilising and everyone's capitulating and we're never going
to see the end of it, only the end of us! Drivel, drivel and
more drivel!

Susanne, a world order has collapsed. When we crossed the
forest that night in the middle of the wood I told the
Countess all that nonsense about the man given up for dead
in order to give her courage – d'you remember? Well it
suddenly became clear to me that I talk to those given up
for dead and that I tell lies when I play the court-jester in
order to plead for my life to the dead and dying. It would
have been better for the Count and Countess if they'd never

crossed the border, if they'd stayed and been murdered – A world order has collapsed, an old world order. The Count and Countess are no longer alive, they just haven't realised it yet. They are laid out on their biers in the Grand Hotel thinking the undertakers are porters, the grave-diggers head-waiters and the layer-out a masseuse. They change their underwear daily but it still remains a shroud, they perfume themselves but they always smell of flowers rotting on a tombstone. They're heading for the grave, Susanne! Is that where you want to go too? I don't.

(ACT I, SCENE IV; PP 104-105)